Artists featured in *Cinema Remixed & Reloaded:*
Black Women Artists and the Moving Image Since 1970

Ina Diane Archer	Bradley McCallum and Jacqueline Tarry
Elizabeth Axtman	Barbara McCullough
Camille Billops	Tracey Moffatt
Carroll Parrott Blue	Wangechi Mutu
María Magdalena Campos-Pons	Senga Nengudi
Zoë Charlton	Michelle Denise Parkerson
Ayoka Chenzira	Jessica Ann Peavy
Ogechi Chieke	Howardena Pindell
Julie Dash	Adrian Piper
Zeinabu irene Davis	Tracey Rose
Stephanie Dinkins	Eve Sandler
Cheryl Dunye	Berni Searle
Debra Edgerton	Xaviera Simmons
Shari Frilot	Lorna Simpson
Colette Gaiter	Cauleen Smith
Leah Gilliam	Pamela Phatsimo Sunstrum
Renée Green	Jocelyn Taylor
Marguerite Harris	Kara Walker
Maren Hassinger	Carrie Mae Weems
Pamela L. Jennings	Yvonne Welbon
Lauren Kelley	Paula Wilson
Yvette Mattern	Lauren Woods

CINEMA REMIXED & RELOADED

Black Women Artists and the Moving Image Since 1970

Andrea Barnwell Brownlee, PhD
Valerie Cassel Oliver

CONTEMPORARY ARTS MUSEUM HOUSTON

SPELMAN COLLEGE MUSEUM OF FINE ART, ATLANTA

Cinema Remixed & Reloaded: Black Women Artists and the Moving Image Since 1970 is coorganized by the Contemporary Arts Museum Houston and the Spelman College Museum of Fine Art, Atlanta.

The exhibition has been made possible by grants from the Fulton County Arts Council under the guidance of the Fulton County Board of Commissioners and the Peter Norton Family Foundation; the Friends of the Spelman College Museum of Fine Art; and by the patrons, benefactors, and donors of the Contemporary Arts Museum Houston's Major Exhibition Fund.

The catalogue accompanying the exhibition *Cinema Remixed & Reloaded: Black Women Artists and the Moving Image Since 1970* has been made possible by a grant from The Brown Foundation, Inc., of Houston.

The audio guide features commentary by Dr. Andrea Barnwell Brownlee, director, Spelman College Museum of Fine Art, and Valerie Cassel Oliver, curator, Contemporary Arts Museum Houston.

NATIONAL ENDOWMENT FOR THE ARTS

TEXAS COMMISSION ON THE ARTS

Continental Airlines

SPELMAN COLLEGE museum OF FINE ART

FULTON COUNTY ARTS COUNCIL

Spelman College

contemporaryartsmuseum houston

Contemporary Arts Museum Houston
Major Exhibition Fund

Major Patron
Fayez Sarofim

Patrons
Chinhui Juhn and Edward R. Allen III
Mr. and Mrs. A. L. Ballard
Mr. and Mrs. I. H. Kempner III
Ms. Louisa Stude Sarofim
Leigh and Reginald R. Smith
Michael Zilkha

Benefactors
Marita and Jonathan B. Fairbanks
George and Mary Josephine Hamman Foundation
Jackson Hicks/Jackson and Company
Elizabeth Howard
King & Spalding, LLP
Elisa J. Stude
The Susan Vaughan Foundation, Inc.

Donors
Anonymous
Anonymous
Baker Botts, LLP
Bergner and Johnson Design
Citi Private Bank
Jana and Richard Fant
Julia and Russell Frankel
Mr. and Mrs. William J. Goldberg/Bernstein Global Wealth Management
Melanie Gray and Mark Wawro
KPMG, LLP
Karol Kreymer and Robert J. Card, MD
Judy and Scott Nyquist
David I. Saperstein
Karen and Harry Susman
Mr. and Mrs. Wallace Wilson

The Contemporary Arts Museum Houston receives partial operating support from the Houston Endowment, Inc., the City of Houston through the Houston Museum District Association, the National Endowment for the Arts, and the Texas Commission on

Patrons of the Spelman College Museum of Fine Art

Director's Circle
Pamela C. Alexander

Platinum Patron
Howard W. Sterling

Gold Patrons
Fannye Hopkins Banks*
SueSue and Bill Bounds
Robert Brawner
Lucinda and Robert Bunnen
Ruby* and Augustus Clay
Charlotte B. Dixon
Jennifer Dossman*
John Eckel, Jr.
Virginia Hepner and Malcolm Barnes
Sivan and Jeff Hines
Thelma Mumford-Glover
Karen Elaine Webster Parks and Ken Parks
Lisa Pinkston
Jay and Arthur Richardson
Candace Smith
Ronda Stryker
Terri Theisen
Regina S. Travis
Lee Davidson Wilder

Bronze Patrons
Beatrice and Isaiah Barnwell
Trojanell Bordenave-Wilson* and Brent Wilson
Edward Brownlee
Wilford Harewood
Amelia Strong Irons*
Tiffani* and Archie Jones
Judy and Scott Lampert
Adrienne Lance Lucas*
Jean and Robert Steele
Virginia Hawkins Stephens*
Clemmie Sanders Tolmaire

*Spelman College Alumna

ESIDENT'S
REWORD

Beverly Daniel Tatum
President
Spelman College

SPELMAN COLLEGE has always believed that visual art is a vital component of a liberal arts education. Since the Spelman College Museum of Fine Art was established in 1996, it has presented first-rate exhibitions that offer students access to the best examples of visual art. The only museum in the nation that focuses on works by and about women of the African Diaspora in its exhibitions and programs, it is uniquely positioned to effect significant change. As the Museum is strategically positioned within the Academic Affairs Division, original exhibitions, such as *Bearing Witness: Work by Contemporary African American Women Artists* (1996), *iona rozeal brown: a³ . . . black on both sides* (2004), and *Amalia Amaki: Boxes, Buttons and the Blues* (2005), help expand the curriculum and encourage students to ask meaningful questions, probe broadly, challenge often, and consider the central and significant contributions of black women artists. While exhibitions enhance the academic programming in important ways, they also appeal to friends of the College as well as viewers who reside throughout metro Atlanta and the region.

Cinema Remixed & Reloaded: Black Women Artists and the Moving Image Since 1970, a daring, bold, innovative exhibition, is no exception. The College is proud to coorganize this landmark survey with the Contemporary Arts Museum Houston (CAMH). I am pleased to acknowledge and thank Linda Shearer, director of CAMH, for this meaningful collaboration. This project, the first to focus on black women artists and video art, was curated by Andrea Barnwell Brownlee, PhD, director of the Museum, and Valerie Cassel Oliver, curator at the CAMH. This historical survey examines an intriguing and unbounded scope of work. Creative projects by such established artists as Camille Billops, Barbara McCullough, Howardena Pindell, and Adrian Piper, who became intrigued with time-based media several decades ago, are presented alongside such midcareer artists as Berni Searle, Lorna Simpson, Kara Walker, and Carrie Mae Weems, who continually garner international acclaim. Works by emerging artists, including Elizabeth Axtman, Debra Edgerton, Lauren Kelley, Jessica Ann Peavy, Pamela Phatsimo Sunstrum, and Lauren Woods, are also featured. While exploring personal experiences and dissecting popular visual culture, the artists in *Cinema Remixed & Reloaded* provide relevant views on several important topics.

In an era of music videos, films, and YouTube, this exhibition resonates directly with Spelman's principal audiences—women of color and video art enthusiasts. While the College community continues to value exhibitions that include such traditional forms as painting, sculpture, and photography, the experimental film, projections, and installations featured in *Cinema Remixed & Reloaded* have invigorated a widespread interest in contemporary artistic practice. Unlike work featured in previous exhibitions, the time-based work requires deliberate and extended time to view, appreciate, and absorb. Contemporary work can be challenging, exhilarating, and, at times, shocking. The exciting body of work presented in this exhibition pushes audiences beyond their limits and requires that they ask new questions of themselves. Moreover, it underscores that black women artists work in a variety of traditional and new media, explore a host of relevant concerns, and warrant and demand a platform to be heard.

Spelman, the optimal place from which to begin this investigation, is proud to be a forerunner in organizing this important exhibition. Together, Dr. Brownlee and Mrs. Cassel Oliver have organized an inspired exhibition, which attests to the enduring talents of many black women artists whose work and perspectives have historically been underexhibited and underdiscussed. Their original and significant contributions to the field and their curatorial vision are potent and impressive. The passion for women artists of the African Diaspora is shared equally by Anne Collins Smith, the curator of collections, who was actively involved in every aspect of the exhibition. Makeba G. Dixon-Hill, the former curato-

This project would not have come to fruition without the ongoing support of the Fulton County Arts Council (FCAC). For more than ten years and especially under the leadership of executive director Veronica Njoku, the FCAC has enthusiastically encouraged several of the Museum's original projects. It is a pleasure to acknowledge the Museum Advisory Board and thank members for their stalwart and central involvement: Fannye Hopkins Banks, Michele Barnett, Robert Brawner, Ruby H. Clay, Terry Comer, Jennifer Dossman, Angela Y. Glover, Virginia Hepner (Special Advisor), James W. Jackson, Susan McLaughlin, Thelma Mumford-Glover, Val Porter, Candace Smith, Regina Travis, and Lee Davidson Wilder.

Several academic departments, especially the Department of Art, the Women's Research and Resource Center, and the English department are particularly supportive of the Museum's efforts, and regularly partner with its staff to organize exhibition-related programs. Faculty and staff, including Ayoka Chenzira, Veta Goler, Beverly Guy-Sheftall, Bahati Kuumba, Arturo Lindsay, Akua McDaniel, Opal Moore, Barbara Nesin, Tarshia Stanley, Sharan Strange, Anne Warner, and Beth-Sarah Wright, are committed to interdisciplinary studies, demonstrate a strong belief in the advancement of the Museum, and help ensure the success of its efforts. For their generosity, in general, and engagement with *Cinema Remixed & Reloaded,* specifically, I am grateful.

Historically, Spelman College has always been a place where black women take flight and soar. *Cinema Remixed & Reloaded: Black Women Artists and the Moving Image Since 1970* and the accompanying exhibition catalogue exemplify the scope of contemporary creativity while honoring this unparalleled history.

IT IS A PRIVILEGE for the Contemporary Arts Museum Houston to collaborate with the Spelman College Museum of Fine Art on this pioneering exhibition, *Cinema Remixed & Reloaded*. Both institutions have been forward-thinking and committed to the presentation and interpretation of work not often found within the mainstream art establishment. Since its founding in 1996, the Spelman Museum has been dedicated to work by and about women of the African Diaspora. The Contemporary Arts Museum Houston opened in 1948 and is celebrating its sixtieth anniversary this year. A noncollecting museum, it consistently has been devoted to the advancement of contemporary art, providing a forum for the research, exhibition, and discussion of new directions in the visual arts. Coorganizing and presenting *Cinema Remixed & Reloaded* is among the meaningful projects that mark the Museum's milestone year.

This Museum has a distinguished history of presenting compelling work by artists from diverse cultural backgrounds. Since her arrival in 2000, Valerie Cassel Oliver has continued this tradition with vigor. As curator, she has been responsible for many groundbreaking solo and group exhibitions, such as *Double Consciousness: Black Conceptual Art Since 1970*, in 2005, and, in 2007, *Black Light / White Noise: Sound and Light in Contemporary Art*, the first comprehensive examination of black artists working in sound and light. *Cinema Remixed & Reloaded* extends this tradition, and I am pleased to acknowledge Valerie and Dr. Andrea Barnwell Brownlee, the exhibition curators. This project has come to fruition because of their vision, time, and passion for this important subject matter, which, until now, has not been the subject of scholarly investigation. I am also delighted to thank and acknowledge Dr. Beverly Daniel Tatum, the president of Spelman College, who has been a fervent champion of the project since its inception and a staunch supporter of

The Contemporary Arts Museum Houston has a strong tradition of featuring artists who examine new media, going back to 1968 with an exhibition of work by Allan Kaprow and Wolf Vostell, two artists who were among the first to originate the idea of the happening. During the 1970s, exhibitions of film, sound art, music, performance, and video took place. Specifically, then director James Harithas organized solo exhibitions of work by such early practitioners of video art as Douglas Davis, Frank Gillette, and Ira Schneider. Gretchen Bender, Bill Viola, Stan Douglas, William Wegman, Eija-Liisa Ahtila & Ann-Sophie Siden, Shirin Neshat, and, most recently, Pipilotti Rist have all been given exhibitions. This chronological listing serves to underscore the Museum's commitment to film and video and its increasing recognition of the important role played by women artists. *Cinema Remixed & Reloaded* further exemplifies this commitment.

We are very pleased to copublish this catalogue, of extensive and scholarly contributions to the field, with the Spelman College Museum of Fine Art. We are also pleased that the Brown Foundation, Inc., of Houston has continued its steady and generous support of our publications program. On behalf of the board of trustees and staff of the Contemporary Arts Museum Houston, I wish to express our deep appreciation for their unstinting support of the Museum and its vital publications program. For a noncollecting museum such as ours, it is the publication that records the event and lives on as a historical document long after the exhibition itself is but a memory.

PREFA

Andrea Barnwell Brownlee, PhD
Director
Spelman College Museum of Fine Art

Valerie Cassel Oliver
Curator
Contemporary Arts Museum Houston

WHEN WE FIRST EMBARKED upon the exhibition project *Cinema Remixed & Reloaded: Black Women Artists and the Moving Image Since 1970,* we were fully aware that it would be a groundbreaking endeavor. Black women had been using the moving image to create work for more than three decades. Much had been published on black women and cinema, yet neither of us could find any evidence of an exhibition that provided a comprehensive overview of the contributions that black women have made and continue to make to video art. Our primary objectives were to chronicle their contributions as well as document their impact on the field. The exhibition project and the corresponding catalogue provided the opportunity to examine and discuss, for the very first time, a collection of forty-three works by two generations of black women video artists who reside throughout the African Diaspora. Their work represents a steady, ongoing effort to explore their lives, evoke familial and communal memories, and critique our social landscape through the use of the moving image within the arenas of cinematic and visual art.

Beyond the cinematic, black women artists have used both film and video as single and multichannel installations, as projections, or as moving images incorporated into sculptural objects, on television, and, more recently, on computer monitors, as well as on the Internet. Regardless of their mode of presentation, what has remained a consistent thematic thread in these works is that it be understood within the contexts of both art and history. As a result, the compendium of works presented in *Cinema Remixed & Reloaded* demonstrates the breadth of concerns these artists have embodied and interrogated over many years, such as the subjugation and liberation of the black body, family, the male gaze, memory, loss, alienation, gender inequities, sexuality, racism, and the pursuit of power. This survey also explores how artists have responded to these issues, developing and honing their responses to correspond to the shifting contemporary landscape.

Video art emerged in the late 1960s as the first portable video cameras were introduced to American consumers. Young artists were drawn to this new medium because video, unlike film, allowed for instantaneous feedback and provided a spontaneous method to create work. In addition, they used the medium to not only defy the traditional conventions of art production but society as well. The medium, with its appeal and familiarity to the masses of viewers, offered an unprecedented level of access, underscoring that the medium itself was the message. Art audiences initially reacted to video with the same reluctance they once had to photography. Critics regarded the new medium as suspect. Despite the early unwillingness to include the medium in the fine arts canon, by the early 1990s video art and film installation work were dominating the international art world. Now, more than thirty years since its emergence, video is widely considered one of the most influential and pervasive genres of contemporary art. It deliberately and effectively incorporates a medium from mainstream culture to engage points of view that often run counter to the cultural norm. Video art provides its audiences with a familiar context in which to mirror and critique historical and contemporary society—and imagine its utopias as well.

Despite widespread recognition for video art and its practitioners, the contributions of many black artists, especially black women artists, have largely gone unrecognized. Although María Magdalena Campos-Pons, Adrian Piper, Berni Searle, Lorna Simpson, Kara Walker, and Carrie Mae Weems have garnered international attention, few black women have drawn the kind of acclaim that has resulted in major, midcareer survey exhibitions. We turned our attention to many artists, both cinematic and visual, who have contributed to the field. We deliberately focused on works by established video, film, and visual artists who began working with the medium in the 1970s, as well as emerging and midcareer artists of the subsequent decades. While several of the featured artists

EFLECTIONS ON ART AS A VERB
Twenty Years Later, in the New Millennium
Interview with Maren Hassinger, Senga Nengudi, and Howardena Pindell

Leslie King-Hammond and Lowery Stokes Sims

DURING THE 1980S, African American artists worked increasingly beyond the traditional boundaries of modernist caucus. The postmodernist idioms of the 1990s would find new vocabularies in the works of these artists. It was at this intersection in history that the exhibition *Art as a Verb—The Evolving Continuum: Installations, Performances, and Videos by 13 Afro-American Artists* became a reality, in 1988. Out of the frustration of the proverbial Black History Month, requests for celebratory presentations, and the urgings of Fred Lazarus, president of the Maryland Institute College of Art (MICA), to create a unique exhibition for his institution, Lowery Stokes Sims and Leslie King-Hammond asked a series of questions, inspired by Betye Saar's megatechno installation *Mojo-Tech* (1986), to test the possibility of an aesthetic presentation that could be embraced beyond the ethnicity of its creators.

The process to define the contextual criteria for this exhibit, which began in 1987, contemplated the rapid advances of technology and its incorporation into the artmaking process. Who would be the artistic leaders of the new millennium? What was the nature or content of the work? How had the body politic, race, class, and gender informed or directed their artmaking in the use of new and nontraditional materials? In the final selection, artists were identified through their consistent and persistent ability to challenge the standard nomenclatures of aesthetics and artistic outcomes in anticipation of the new millennium. Charles Abramson, David Hammons, Maren Hassinger, Candace Hill-Montgomery, Martha Jackson-Jarvis, Senga Nengudi, Lorraine O'Grady, Howardena Pindell, Adrian Piper, Faith Ringgold, Betye Saar, and Joyce Scott became the architects who activated and articulated a multimedia exhibit that came to be known as *Art as a Verb*.

It was an amazing and remarkable experience, heightened by the fact that there was no confirmed checklist. All the works were created on-site specifically for this exhibition. It was as much an adventure and journey for the artists to explore and test new terrain as it was for the curators to respond and interpret.

Howardena Pindell, still from *Free, White and 21*, 1980

In the twenty years since *Art as a Verb,* questions have been asked about a second exhibition. On the occasion of *Cinema Remixed & Reloaded: Black Women Artists and the Moving Image Since 1970,* we asked Maren Hassinger, Senga Nengudi, Howardena Pindell, and Adrian Piper to participate in an online conversation about their use of digital, video, and film mediums in their work during the past twenty years. The following excerpts revisit a potent period in history for these artists and the curators. (Adrian Piper declined, given the time constraints of a demanding project in Germany.)

Lowery Stokes Sims: What inspired your first use of video as a medium to explore your artistic vision?

Howardena Pindell: I'm basically a painter and never really thought of using video. What I found difficult were all the technical glitches you have—just getting the equipment, the equipment having problems, if it's too hot, too cold, and just the expense of the equipment. But I had this idea that came to me after I was in that car accident. (I had a head injury; at least that was one of my injuries. I had a concussion, and that's part of the reason why I wrapped my head in the video; it was an unconscious reference to the car accident.) It was so strong, this idea about having myself in a blonde wig . . . I went to Woolworth's; Woolworth's was then on 34th Street, before the whole Woolworth's chain closed down. The sunglasses I had from when I was a child, so those are authentic 1950s sunglasses; maybe they're from the '60s, I don't know. I gathered all my materials together, and I got some stage makeup; I had this idea, and it was so strong I couldn't shake it. The last thing I would have done my regular work in is video, but this one had to be video. I don't remember who I talked to, but I was contacted by the woman at Downtown Community Television. She had some camerawomen who would love to film

it for me. She brought them to my loft on 7th Avenue and 28th Street. The big problem was the noise outside, because I was close to the subway. The stop was right at 28th Street. There was a lot of street traffic, but we did it anyway. I bought some photography backdrop paper so I would have different colors in the background. Then, there was the question of what to wear. My mother was always buying and sending me clothes—stuff I didn't like. I thought, I'll use the clothes for the video. So, I changed my clothes during the course of the video. The impulse was, mainly, I had this idea and couldn't shake it; it wouldn't go away. I inquired around, and I was offered camera people, and I took it. They also helped with editing the piece I called *Free, White and 21.*

Maren Hassinger: One of my first projects was *daily mask,* a 16mm film transferred to video. I always loved movies and TV. I wanted to make a movie. Obviously, I couldn't afford a Hollywood film in any of its manifestations; that set me thinking about something quite short, but not animated. I could be the actor. The story could be my story. I could reference African sculpture, art history (modern and postmodern), social and cultural history, feminist issues, and aesthetics. I don't know exactly how all these ideas gelled into *daily mask,* but I can tell you I knew I was onto something when a viewer wanted to know if I was a man! It is such a simple idea. I feel it embodies a potential for growth and healing if we examine it and understand the uselessness of stereotyping—masking that obscures our humanity and commonality.

Senga Nengudi: I only struck up a romance with video about two years ago, with the beginning of a residency at the Fabric Workshop and Museum (FWM), in Philadelphia. That residency allowed me the time, technical assistance, and equipment to tackle my first video project. It always seemed out of my reach as a creative tool because of cost and technological savvy. I have always preferred the still camera. Perhaps "still" tells the story. With a photo, one is able to meditate on the image and let it reveal its story to you. There is the opportunity to be an active participant in filling in the narrative.

Leslie King-Hammond: Were there any particular artists or individuals who provided some insight, support, or references for your work?

HP: I was actually totally ignorant about video. A lot of the few things I saw—I was not a video aficionado—were very narcissistic and self-involved. I guess mine was, too, in a way. But there weren't any individuals, other than the woman from Downtown Community Television and the two camerawomen, that helped me with the tape. In fact, I mention it in an article from my book that had been printed originally in *Third Text,* London. When the woman who helped me sent it to a festival, they rejected it; they said it was too divisive. I guess they felt it attacked white folks.

MH: I wouldn't have made this without the support of friends. My friend (and former student) the artist and gallerist David Allen (now Ford Allen) produced *daily mask*. He was on set at all times, encouraging me and suggesting solutions. He was the one who told me how I might use the lighting in the final shot to bring the piece to a conclusion. He also— and I can't thank him enough for this—brought along his pal David Flanigan to shoot it. David Flanigan has gone on to shoot independent films and episodes of *The Wire,* aired on HBO. My good friend Christian Majcherski, a writer, who has built his own magnificent houses, found the vanity-table prop near his home in Vermont and trucked it all the way back to the studio in Wainscot, Long Island. LTV provided the studio space, because I had been renting editing facilities there for some time.

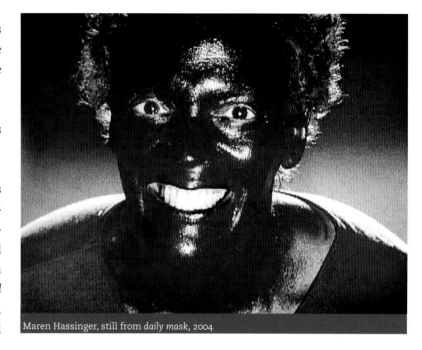

Maren Hassinger, still from *daily mask*, 2004

We committed *daily mask* to 16mm film on a cool afternoon in February (I believe) of 1997.

The editing went on for years and actually spanned the Western Hemisphere. It began after I moved to Baltimore and met a graduate photography student at MICA, Lori Kimboro. We discussed lots of ideas, and how to incorporate music from my friend in Hampton Bays. This music is very interesting. I knew about it because I was taking an African dance class from Susan Bailey. Her husband, Andrew, and his band (of changing musicians) accompanied the class. Andrew and Susan Bailey were born in South Africa. They are white. When Lori graduated, the editing was still up in the air. Then, along comes Donna Conlon, one of my students at Rinehart School of Graduate Sculpture. She began her studies as an undergraduate in science. When she came to Rinehart, she hoped to become a sculptor; she left as a sculptor/video artist with the emphasis on video, and collections of cultural significance. Her videos have been screened internationally, notably in the 2005 Venice Biennale. Donna finished the edit in Panama with absolute sensitivity. She noticed that in the opening shot I swallowed and inhaled, and that's when the film begins. What an eye she has.

SN: My wonderful peers continue to provide insight, support, and stimulation: Linda Goode Bryant, David Hammons, Maren Hassinger, Barbara McCullough, John Outterbridge, and others not so well known are always searching, moving forward to the next frontier. That includes Charles Abramson and Noah Purifoy, who are no longer on this plane. Whatever the medium of presentation, these renegades infuse their work with cultural importance, visual grace, and *knuf* [funk]. I must say that until two years ago—zero. Technology was only a means to an end, with that end being the documentation of my work.

LSS: How important were video and digital technology in the experimentation or exploration of ideas about imaging, performance, narrative, or personal introspection?

HP: Actually, video and digital technology were not in the uppermost part of my mind; I'm a painter, and I was more interested in painting. But this seemed the right medium for this expression, so . . . for this idea, I chose it. But I didn't pursue it—except I got a small grant to do a video workshop with the Kitchen, and I was able to do a short tape called *Doubling,* which was about war atrocities. It was only a two- or three-minute tape. I did that, I believe, in the mid-1990s. (I have to check my résumé for that date.) It had to do with the Kitchen granting artists time and their adventurous editor. They helped us edit our tape, and then gave us a little performance time. They had a program of our tapes, which were shown on Downtown Community Television—so it was also aired publicly.

MH: I've thought a lot about the differences between my sculptures and the moving image pieces. What I believe is this: My sculptures tend to have a greater degree of abstraction, even though early works often reference nature and recent works include self-portrait masks. The film/video pieces are like newsreels. They're real. The viewer doesn't have to make so many conceptual leaps. There is a familiarity that comes from generations of us watching TV and movies. Information can be quickly exchanged and digested.

SN: There has been a lot of water under the bridge since *Art as a Verb.* I continue to follow the line of Art as Action, creating installations that satisfy my aesthetic leanings and allow me to follow my creative visioning, and show the course of my human development, concerns, and philosophy. I do love the power and flexibility of digital photography. Its editing capability has no parallel at this time for me. As Propecia Leigh, I create photographic essays covering "mise-en-scènes" of remembrances.

I'm still working on errant footage that was shot during my FWM residency, entitled *The Threader.* Just the opposite of my *Warp Trance* video, which is abstract rhythmic sounds and visuals of fabric-mill production. In the work, "The Threader," Amir, a worker, is followed while performing the ritual—his very specific task—of winding thread in the preparation of making tassels and trims for such clients as the White House. Amir is an employee of the famed Scalamandre Fabric Mill, in Queens, New York, and is exemplary of workers in these sometimes turn-of-the-century factory mills. They do the same task many times a day, every day, for years on end, consistent in their quality control and proud of the end product.

Senga Nengudi, still from *The Threader*, 2007

So, I did start using TV or video—not as a video medium but as a kind of support. That is, I photographed it so it was really photography as opposed to video. And I'm still doing them. I've included text with them; I had my War Series back in the 1980s. I did use video, but not in the sense of using the medium per se; I just used it as a vehicle. I'll put it that way. But in the 1990s—my mother died in '91—I started doing a lot of memorials. The pieces created since then have been mainly slavery memorials, and a memorial to my mother, which dealt with mother love and hate, because my mother and I didn't really get along that well. In the slavery memorials from 1993, I started working with colored sand and doing installations in colored sand. I've done three of those—two of them slavery memorials, and in one of them I worked with children and children's drawings in Hartford, Connecticut, at the Charter Oak Cultural Center. I haven't done any sand pieces since 2000. I'm getting old and it's hard to be on your knees on the floor all day. I suppose I could do another one.

LKH: Since *Art as a Verb,* what other works have you created? What are you working on now that incorporates or references the technologies of digital or video imaging?

HP: Actually, nothing! After 1988, the major painting I created was *Scapegoat,* which the Studio Museum in Harlem owns. But there's nothing that I did after that, except the workshop at the Kitchen, where I used digital or video imaging. Oh, it just dawned on me: I forgot my video drawings! Good Lord! In 1972–73, I started working with television, but I used photography as my medium. I was photographing TV, making drawings on acetate, and putting them on the TV set and photographing them. That started in 1972–73, and I'm still doing them. In fact, I'm working on a set that are going to be shown in Berlin in about a month.

MH: Currently, I'm in a show called *At Freedom's Door: Challenging Slavery in Maryland.* In this show, I have a piece called *Legacy,* which incorporates video text projected onto an archival photo and music. I wanted to document this piece in video. The person I asked to shoot the video thought the piece had significance and wanted to make a documentary, narrative-style movie. Now that's happening, and I have a role in the endeavor. That's like two pieces for the price of one. Since *Art as a Verb,* I've made lots of pieces—some shown, some not. I made lots of landscapes. I made a comedy-documentary about a dummy (literally mannequin) traffic cop in East Hampton (where I lived for six years). I danced for the camera. I recorded the play of sunlight on surfaces in my home in Baltimore. I've used the camera to describe my surroundings since about 1991.

'OWER TO THE PEOPLE
Video's Legacy as a Medium for Social Change

Merrill Falkenberg

FROM ITS INCEPTION in the late 1960s, video art has been utilized by artists and activists committed to challenging established hierarchies and effecting social change. The portable video camera, first introduced in 1965, opened up new possibilities for documentation, surveillance, and information transmission through its unprecedented ability to record in real time. Whereas photography and film required elaborate processing, video's intrinsic principle was feedback, as users could simultaneously respond to and alter their image onscreen. This type of immediacy had particular appeal for performance artists, such as Bruce Nauman, Vito Acconci, and Joan Jonas, as they could record their often solitary activities in the studio for broader audiences. During video's first decade, the notion of feedback had further resonance in political terms. Emerging during a period of pervasive dissatisfaction with both the government and the media's representation of the Vietnam War, video offered the promise of an alternative

Adrian Piper, still from *Cornered*, 1988

source of broadcast programming, enabling additional voices to be heard. In *Cinema Remixed & Reloaded: Black Women Artists and the Moving Image Since 1970*, Howardena Pindell's 1980 video *Free, White and 21* and Adrian Piper's 1988 installation *Cornered* merge the activist and artistic impulses behind video's origins. These artists continue video's legacy, both as a means to solicit a greater level of engagement from the viewer and as a medium for recording resistance.

Video was immediately distinguished by its interactive capabilities. The invention of the term "interactivity," first introduced in a 1967 electronics textbook, roughly coincides with the production of the first portable video cameras. Originally a technical description to explain the relationship between a computer and a user, interactivity soon was redefined in ways that reflected both technological and social connotations. On the one hand, the notions of a reciprocal circuit of exchange between person and machine coalesced with the popular writings of mathematician Norbert Weiner, inventor Buckminster Fuller, and media theorist

Berger points out, in linguistics the index is a figure of speech that serves as a pointer, literally directing the subject of a sentence or phrase to the particular object, phenomenon, or place. The words "this," "you," and "here" are indexes. By using the term "you" and shifting the locale of the aesthetic experience from a distant "there" to an immediate "here," Piper locates the viewer and the art object in the same time frame. Both, in effect, are operating in real, immediate time; neither history nor transcendence is allowed to intervene in the aesthetic experience.[4] While Piper uses this technique in most of her texts and live performances, the real time of the video further emphasizes this effect.

Both Pindell and Piper use video's interactive potential to speak to an invisible white audience that symbolically represents the racism and oppression to which both artists have been subjected. Video's ability to record in real time and thus enable the artist to work independently of a large production crew is particularly conducive to performances intended to provoke a deeper level of engagement from the viewer. Co-opting video's legacy for social change, both Pindell and Piper use the medium to continue the tradition established by video's first generation of users. They provide an alternative to mainstream media structures and the oppressive narratives they promote, while expanding the discourse of video art's first decade, to examine issues of racial and gender bias.

NOTES

1. Fredric Jameson, "End of Art or End of History?" in *The Cultural Turn: Selected Writings on the Postmodern, 1983–1998* (New York: Verso, 1998), 75.

2. Dan Graham, *Rock My Religion* (Cambridge, Mass.: MIT Press, 1993), 52.

3. Maurice Berger, *Adrian Piper: A Retrospective* (New York: D.A.P. Press, 1999), 28.

4. Ibid.

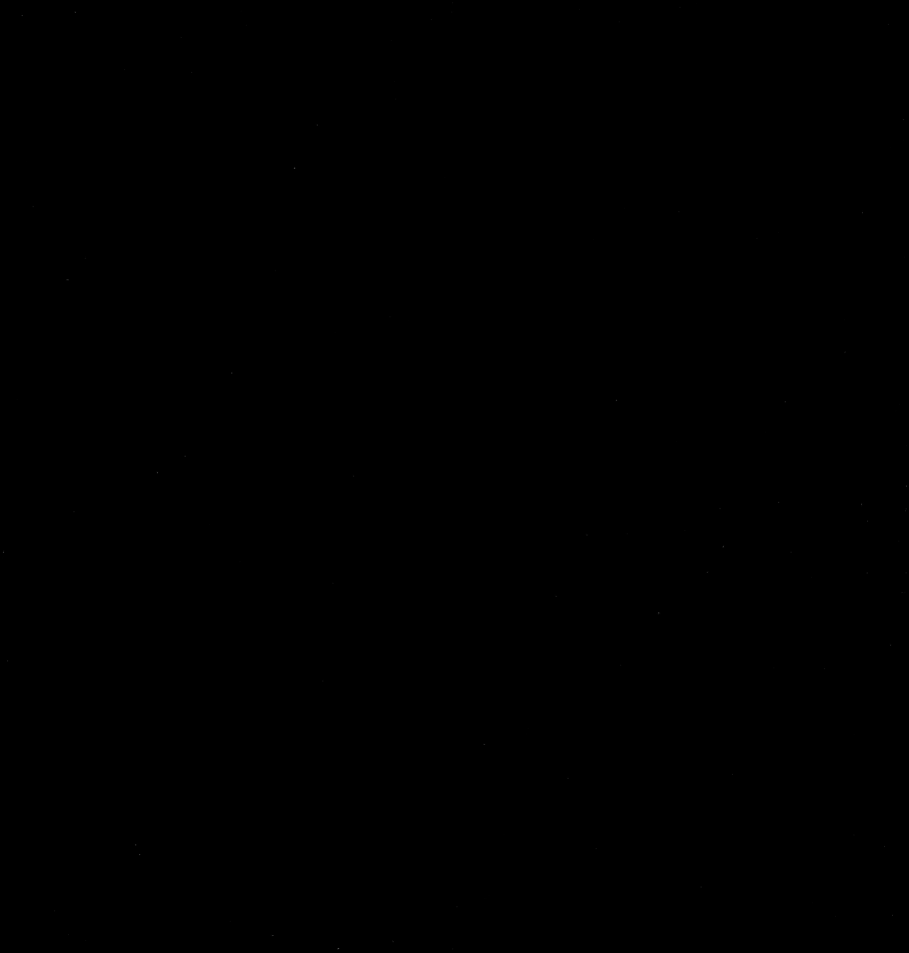

AMATEURISM & AUTEURISM
Contrary Instincts in Black Women's Experimental Film Forms

Romi Crawford

WOMEN'S WORK HAS BEEN historically discounted, and black women's labors, for love or money, need special attention to gain recognition. Mostly, this has been a matter of not valuing, or ignoring, forms within forms. Just as women's writing existed prior to the first novel by a woman being published—in the form of overlooked diaries, letters, captivity narratives, etc.—scant critical interest was shown to these forms before the 1970s. These were mostly overlooked until feminist initiatives (professional groundswells of the movement) ushered in new modes of interpreting and appreciating these new (old) forms. Part of the same literary idea and imagination, these *minor* works, defined as writing acts that countered dominant narrative forms, were considered *petite* offerings; by this I mean stylistically transient, ephemeral, and brief, when compared to the grander gestures of male-authored literary works. Within the African American tradition, a similar instantiation of a vernacular form is articulated by the writer Alice Walker, who, in a seminal work from 1974, encourages black women readers to go "in search of our mothers' gardens." In effect, she implores us to recognize, and see, the creative work of our mothers, grandmothers, and, by the time of this writing, great-grandmothers—despite the paucity of identifiable artifacts. She describes her mother as being one of these women, as an "artist who left her mark in the only materials she could afford and the only medium her position in society allowed her to use."[1]

Walker's approach, looking beyond the iconic forms, such as literature and painting, to new (old) forms, like gardens and quilts, enabled a generation of willing cultural readers—men and women, black and white alike—to comprehend the polyformal potential of the creative voice. Our black mothers' gardens, like our white mothers' diaries, were no less viable as artistic forms. But the minor scale, the reduced financial worth, the failure to offer up generalized and grand truths, has made these seem like lesser works, slight and seemingly inconsequential compared to

Ayoka Chenzira, still from *Hair Piece: A Film for Nappyheaded People*, 1985

Despite the stalled training opportunities within Hollywood—we still lack a female director with market value or critical stature to rival male film artists—black women forged ahead and continue to work in experimental film modes. Many of the nonnarrative or short-form practitioners have forged an alternative path to gaining skills and experience. They have secured professional status by credentialing with MFA programs, and then going on to work in academic settings.[15]

A profession in film for black and nonblack makers alike was, until recently, a matter of work-based training and/or mentorship. The University of Southern California School of Cinematic Arts was established as early as 1929, but formal degree programs did not gain real momentum until much later, in the 1970s and '80s. "Since the 1970s, film degrees have increased nearly 300 percent." It is purported that by 1989, "35 percent of all first-time directors had attended film school, and that by 1992, the figure had increased to 72 percent."[16]

The style of Hollywood film is not the only thing that has been impacted by the popularity of MFA programs. Experimental pioneer Stan Brakhage dropped out of school to make films, but later taught the subject to help sustain his career as a nonnarrative filmmaker. Similarly, black women who make experimental films have trained in film programs and found careers in the teaching sector as a way to work around the limitations of big-budget filmmaking and the aesthetic codings that result from it. Although some believe that black women filmmakers since the 1970s are untrained amateurs, the facts reveal a connection to film schools and MFA programs, and a more strategic implementation of amateur modalities. Jacqueline Bobo astutely points out:

> Black women have earned master of arts degrees from prestigious graduate film and television programs—such as Columbia University, UCLA, USC, Chicago Institute of the Arts, Northwestern—and many have undergraduate degrees from NYU, Howard, Temple, and San Francisco State University. Thus, Black women's works demonstrate the makers' thorough understanding of cinema and media history, theory, and criticism, which is reflected in the exemplary quality of their films and videos.[17]

In the ten years since Bobo's observation, an even broader array of institutions have served as training grounds for black women experimentalists, who often use their skills and expertise to craft—radically, rather than tragically—*little* films. Not unlike other waves of experimental and avant-garde cinema, black women filmmakers worked not only against but, more significantly, beyond the normative technological and monetary trappings and advantages of commercial and Hollywood cinema.

Cheryl Dunye's early, short-form, on-the-cheap videos are a mash of documentary, autobiography, and fiction. In such films as *Janine* (1990), she self-references and self-authorizes to the extent that she becomes her own text.[18] Similarly, Yvonne Welbon's video biographies from the 1990s reveal the "unexpected importance"[19] of minimized subjectivities. *Monique* (1991) and *Living with Pride: Ruth C. Ellis @ 100* (1999), a documentary on the oldest-known living black lesbian, assert the significance of microsubjective knowledges. Welbon and Dunye's videos from this period disclose a broad epistemological value, even as they emerge from a limited range of materials and technologies. Roland Barthes's description of the unskilled striptease act helps to elucidate the impact of these low-tech procedures:[20]

> Few disguises as a starting point—gauche steps, unsatisfactory dancing, girls constantly threatened by immobility, and above all by a "technical" awkwardness (the resistance of briefs, dress or bra) which gives to the gestures of unveiling an unexpected importance . . .[21]

Cauleen Smith, still from *The Changing Same*, 1998–2001

Limitations produce innovations in the cinema arts in much the same way that grand feats of financial and technological prowess help to activate and renew the form. Working in low-tech materials and stock, such as 8mm and Super 8; employing fast cuts, under cuts, and hybrid editing; using port-a-packs and handheld cameras; and bringing a handmade or artisanal quality to the process—these are just some of the minoritizing strategies that experimental film- and videomakers have used to heighten the experience of inventiveness. Reduced means have also influenced modes of reception:

> As the dominant and industrial cinema achieved higher production values and greater spectacle, the avant-garde affirmed its "otherness" in cheap, personal and "amateur" films which circulated outside the cinema chains. . . . The gallery or club rather than the movie-house is their site, outside the space and conventions of cinema.[22]

For black women filmmakers, working *small*, with compromising materials and in residual spaces, is no less heroic. Actually, it demonstrates their awareness of the medium's social, formal, and aesthetic histories—all of which avail an appreciation for the medium's unaggrandizing aspects. For instance, the social history of film reveals the little-theater movement of the 1920s, which challenged the overabundance of Hollywood-style offerings at theaters, creating art-house spaces as an antidote. The formal history of film is replete with accidental developments. And the aesthetic history of film is advanced by the wayward or part-time involvements of painters, sculptors, and photographers.

Annette Kuhn claims that "low investments of money and 'professionalism' have meant that avant-garde cinema has historically been much more open than the film industry to women."[23] Inverting this statement describes more precisely the role of black women. Black women filmmakers have been much more receptive to avant-garde rather than industry strategies in the creation of their films. They are seldom included in the histories or canons of avant-gardism. Yet, despite this, they are open to its logic and modes of investigation. Perhaps, then, we should interpret *small* acts—at the level of subject, material, and venue selection—as informed practices rather than naive behaviors.

How black people and, especially, black women demonstrate the will and desire for power is an underdiscussed topic. The history of African American progress and ambition is peppered with biocritical proofs of black women's will to authority and creative strength. Sojourner Truth, Harriet Tubman, Madame C. J. Walker, and Eloyce Gist are but a few examples, and in our contemporary era Oprah Winfrey stands out as a formidable *powerhouse*. With the start of the 1970s black feminist movement, women gained recognition, for the first time perhaps, as agents of knowledge. In fact, black feminism existed prior to the 1970s through the work of nineteenth- and early-twentieth-century evangelists, educators, suffragists, abolitionists, and artists. At best, the 1970s signaled a renewed possibility for the voice and vision of black women. A fresh scene of writers and poets arose; black studies and feminist studies programs emerged at universities, and black women, who had always been workers, ventured into professional, rather than domestic, paths. All of this brought confidence and affirmation to a realm of knowledge and information that was traditionally quieted and undercover.

The undisclosed nature of black American creativity has historical basis. Slaves had limited expressive freedom and were not allowed to read or write. This did not suppress creative endeavor, but it did curb their confidence in allowing witness to these forms. Instead of aggrandizing their creative efforts, they let them subsist—as part of a group, collective, or social phenomenon—and in doing so, they obviated individual authorship. One might say that they offered a generalized, in lieu of an individuated, talent.

Much is said about the repercussions that ensue in black American expressive experience as a result of being denied the opportunity to read and write, but less is said about how the denial of authorship (with a capital *A*) has affected the black creative tradition. Not only were black Americans barred from the act of writing, but this, in turn, made the more grandiose prerogative of authorship impossible. For this reason, the idea of auteurship, in relation to black filmmakers, remains almost unspoken. Spike Lee, John Singleton, and Melvin Van Peebles have been able to carve out a noticeable and definable surface aesthetic, predicated on participating in several aspects of filmmaking, but we can also speak to the concept of auteurism when discussing black women's experimental practices. Although not an obvious auteuristic cinema, it follows from similar precepts.

The method of auteurism is distinct from, but related to, the notion of authorship. It derives from the French word for "author," but imposes a more consummated personal imprint onto the film text. The auteur theory also encourages an interesting conflation of the writer's pen and filmmaker's camera. Alexandre Astruc's concept of the camera-stylo, or "camera-pen,"[24] suggests that film directors use their cameras like writers use their pens, to make work that is not overwrought by the collective vision that results from a team of film workers.

Henry Louis Gates has indicated how the path from slavery to freedom was, in part, fueled by the slave's learning, despite sanctions against it, to read and write. For instance, in penning his own manumission papers, Frederick Douglass was halfway to changing his condition from slave to freed man. The move to literacy for blacks created authors along the way; writing acts, in turn, allowed them to become authors. But it is film that truly encourages, and presses the full significance of, the auteur mode for black artists.

A. L. Rees points out that the "post avant-garde–fragmentation and sound montage in Spike Lee, John Akomfrah, and Isaac Julien were used to convey black urban experience."[25] Unlike the black male auteur, who arrives at voice, vision, and a look by employing fragmentation and insurgent musical forms, the black female video-filmmaker derives authority by promoting a desire, first and foremost, for self-revelation. What connects Welbon and Dunye's videos to the filmic works of Camille Billops, Ayoka Chenzira, and Julie Dash is the way the projects demonstrate a similar desire for what Kaja Silverman calls "female authorial voice."[26]

Stemming actively or passively from the possibilities generated from the black feminist movement, their experiments in moving-image techniques point to a "desire for complete recognition and understanding of black women's life experiences as valuable, complex, and diverse."[27]

This experimental film and video is instructive in how it contradicts its own aspirations and desires. As a living genre, it negotiates two *competing* aesthetic inclinations—the will to make courageous and huge observations on pertinent social issues, and the desire to work through a method of minor subjects and small procedures. It reveals the largesse of black feminist consciousness—as a useful domain for critical-filmic inquiry and investigation. Yet, it also *settles* for under- rather than overproduced works, preferring this version of authorial personality to the divested self-interest that results from mainstream dictates of technique and style. Black women's experimental cinema demonstrates such paradox and "contrary instincts." This conjunction of macro and micro tendencies is one of the genre's most distinguishing signs.

NOTES

1. Alice Walker, *In Search of Our Mothers' Gardens* (New York: Harcourt Brace, 1984), 239.

2. Experimental film and cinema is variously defined, but generally pertains to filmmaking practices that differ from those of the traditional Hollywood film style. While the Hollywood film style is built upon narrative order, complementary and logical editing, and technical precision, experimental film as a genre demonstrates an openness to nonchronological and poetic editing, using outmoded film stock and video and manipulating the film and video with handmade processes. The genre is dependent upon alternative modes of distribution and dissemination as it has less inherent entertainment value than mainstream cinema.

3. The works were seen mostly by other like-minded women filmmakers, and, as Cheryl Dunye points out, the format and short-format style did not appeal to a diverse range of black viewers. She mentions, in an interview, that her interest in making a feature-length film stems from a desire to show her work to a wider black audience.

4. See A. L. Rees, *A History of Experimental Film and Video* (London: British Film Institute, 1999), 93–96.

5. Ibid.

6. Expertise in this sense is connected to self-proficiency.

7. Walker, *Mothers' Gardens*, 235.

8. Ibid., 235–36.

9. A black feminism implies its own double consciousness, in the DuBoisian sense, and informs the project of black women's experimental film. I borrow the phrase from Patricia Hill Collins; see Collins, *Black Feminist Thought: Knowledge, Consciousness, and the Politics of Empowerment* (Boston: Unwin Hyman, 1990), 221–38.

10. Rees, *History*, 93–96.

11. David Bordwell and Kristin Thompson, *Film History* (New York: McGraw Hill, 2002).

12. Pearl Bowser has recovered much of this history of the pioneers of black women's film. See Jacqueline Bobo, ed., *Black Women Film and Video Artists* (New York: Routledge, 1988), 3–21.

13. Ibid.

14. B. Denise Hawkins, "Flocking to Film School—Minorities and the Film Industry," *Black Issues in Higher Education*, January 11, 1996.

15. Black women experimental filmmakers, including Pamela L. Jennings, Cheryl Dunye, Yvonne Welbon, and Shari Frilot, all had connections to the academy as a significant site for their training and professional development.

16. Hawkins, "Flocking to Film School."

17. Bobo, *Black Women*, xi.

18. Dunye is quoted in an interview as saying, "I become my own text." See *Women of Vision: Histories in Feminist Film and Video*, ed. Alexandra Juhasz (Minneapolis: University of Minnesota Press, 2001), 293.

19. Roland Barthes, "Strip-Tease," in *Mythologies* (New York: Hill and Wang, 1972), 84–88.

20. Ibid.

21. Ibid.

22. Rees, *History*, 2.

23. Lauren Rabinowitz, "The Woman Filmmaker in the New York Avant-Garde," in *Experimental Cinema: The Film Reader*, ed. Wheeler Winston Dixon and Gwendolyn Audrey Foster (London: Routledge, 2002), 74.

24. Alexandre Astruc, "The Birth of a New Avant-Garde: La Camera-Stylo," in *The New Wave*, ed. Peter Graham (London: Secker & Warburg, 1968), 17–23.

25. Rees, *History*, 105–6.

26. As Kaja Silverman has pointed out, we might consider how "female authorial desire" is constructed, despite even Barthes's 1968 proclamation of the author's death or demise; see Silverman, *The Acoustic Mirror: The Female Voice in Psychoanalysis and Cinema* (Bloomington: Indiana University Press, 1988), 87–88.

27. Gloria Gibson, "Black Women's Independent Cinema," in *Experimental Cinema*, 314.

BETWEEN ARTIFICE & AUTHENTICITY
The Black Female Body in Performance

Valerie Cassel Oliver

THE HISTORY OF ARTIFICE / THE ART OF RESISTANCE

The black female body, even in the nascent years of the twenty-first century, remains a space of corporeal contestation. This contestation has been fueled, in part, by fictional narratives that have served to supplant an authentic, complex state of being. Beginning with the ethnographic photographs at the outset of the nineteenth century, the dark female body became entangled with fictional narratives that emerged out of the socioeconomic space of slavery and colonization. In the aftermath of these historical periods, society has been left to deconstruct the fiction surrounding the black female body, even though such fictionalizations continue. In today's society, however, ethnographic photographs have been replaced by images on billboards and in magazines or in rap videos and films, in which the black female body performs predictable fictions for viewers. Ironically, even though the technology of rendering the body has advanced, the context in which it is often presented has only marginally evolved.

After nearly five hundred years of encounters with the European, the black female body is still largely imagined. Contemporary society, as a whole, is no closer to discerning her authentic womanhood from the fictionalized. This is because popular culture—especially movies, television programs, even music videos—serves only to offer exaggerated fictional narratives that range from the video-vixen and sexual-conquest scenario to the overweight, angry, unwed mother of five living on welfare, to the domineering and oppressive wife, to the Harvard-educated, upper-middle-class professional who still *can't get a man*. There is a perceived legitimacy to this fiction, due mostly to the performance of black bodies, and as such, their implied complicity. Even black women have been duped into adapting this fiction as a mirror of self-reflection. But fictionalization, while problematic to the black psyche, is not solely a black issue. Because cinema and television are, by design

Kara Walker, still from *8 Possible Beginnings or: The Creation of African-America, a Moving Picture by Kara E. Walker*, 2005 fiction, it has seeped into the psyche of those consistently bombarded with ethnic as well as gender stereotypes. What makes black women so insidiously vulnerable to this industry is that even fictional portrayals often underscore a European impression (read *stereotype*) of black womanhood. Given the history of slavery and European imperialism in Africa, the ability for black people to define themselves cogently is, time and again, supplanted. Fictions offer little to no insight into the complex realities of black womanhood, nor do they provide discursive meditations on the black female body, whose very corporeal being is, historically and psychologically, rooted in voiceless oppression. And yet, there has been a history of resistance to this state of voicelessness.

Even in the oppressive era of slavery, the black female resisted stereotypes and fictional portrayals through her own words, which authentically chronicled her life and struggles. Early black literature attests to such resistance, especially narratives and novels written by former slaves who successfully escaped to freedom. One such novel, by Harriet Jacobs, is particularly insightful. Writing under the pseudonym Linda Brent, Jacobs was quick to note in her novel *The Deeper Wrong; or, Incidents in the Life of a Slave Girl* that the work is no fictional account. In the introduction, she writes, "Reader, be assured this narrative is no fiction. I am aware that some of my adventures may seem incredible; but they are, nevertheless, strictly true."[1] In the twentieth century, nearly one hundred years after Jacobs's novel, black women were still resisting the fictional renderings of them as depicted in film and televised programs of the day.

Beyond race films (written, directed, and produced by blacks, with black performers and for black audiences) and ethnographic portraits of black communities created by black anthropologists like Zora Neale Hurston, portrayals of black people, especially women, were largely fictional, written and oftentimes performed by whites. It was not until 1950, when ABC first aired *Beulah,* the radio show turned sitcom, that a nationally televised program featured a black actor in a leading role. *Beulah* ran for three years before being canceled. Although the program featured such lauded and popular actors as Ethel Waters, Hattie McDaniel, and Louise Beavers in the title role, the character of Beulah bordered on the iconic Mammy stereotype and did little to deconstruct the fiction surrounding the black female body or advance the struggle for civil rights. After the cancellation of *Beulah,* positive images of black men and women in leading, nonmusical roles were infrequent in mainstream media until 1968, when NBC launched *Julia,* starring Diahann Carroll. The program was groundbreaking: for the first time, a black woman was featured—and celebrated—in a nonstereotypical lead role. However groundbreaking, the program's episodes rarely reflected the realities of black life in the United States in the late 1960s.[2] The tension that existed between the placid artifice of show and a gritty reality was palpable. In 1968, the war in Vietnam was escalating, as were protests; Martin Luther King, Jr., had been assassinated, as had Robert Kennedy; and the American landscape was radically shifting in the wake of social upheaval. Black Americans, understandably distrustful of the cultural hegemony of mainstream media, were no longer content to accept fictionalized depictions of themselves. Along with a mass engagement of political advocacy, a call was made to self-define black culture, standards of beauty, and history. Given the accessibility of video technology on the consumer market, blacks were eager to record their own stories, from intimate portraits of family life to political rallies. Technology became an essential element in creating alternative images of black life, ones previously unseen or anticipated in mainstream media. The moving image also turned the tables on a forced depiction of blackness; clearly, this was resistance. Black female filmmakers, writers, directors, and visual artists used the medium to challenge the overt fictional portrayals in modern society and to create more authentic projections of black womanhood.

While there is documentation of the existence of black women film-makers during the late 1930s and '40s, it would not be until the advances in video technology in the early 1960s that a proliferation of black women began chronicling their own authentic selves. Buoyed by the early radical practices of video artists, whose very use of the medium was to usurp and agitate the status quo, a young generation of black artists, many of whom attended the University of California, Los Angeles, film program, paid heed. Although their subsequent works did not mimic the early video practices of Bruce Nauman (body as mechanical) or Vito Acconci (action/happenings), there was an immediate connection to the presence of the body in performance.

The black body once again becomes an imperative form of resistance. Often, artists used their bodies in performance, to authenticate their own narratives as a signifier of resistance—very much like the words of Harriet Jacobs. This act was to have a significant influence on future generations of experimental filmmakers and visual artists alike, who, subsequently, used their bodies as both material and metaphor. The very presence of the black female body in performance evokes such dichotomies as bondage and liberation, vulnerability and empowerment, lure and loathing, among a host of other binaries derived from a history of oppression and the struggle to stem its insidious effect. Incredible as it may sound, transcending the fiction to arrive at a place of authenticity lies not only in the ability to absorb the fictional (because truth is often interwoven in fiction) but to do so without being reduced to, or rendered as, fiction. This metaphysical exchange has not only defined the black experience historically but also the struggle toward authenticity.[3] The black body is, after all, a nexus of confounding identities, composed of layers upon layers of fiction and the anonymity or unknowingness of self

that resulted from slavery.[4] This unknowingness is only counterbalanced by the residual of lives lived, what can be traced and authenticated, as well as through present-day existences. The black body in performance becomes essential in affirming one's individual and collective presence; it also proves vital in revealing the complexities of black womanhood beyond the stereotypical depictions. Since the late 1960s, black women filmmakers and video and visual artists, have presented their authentic selves to the viewer. They have sought not only to write, direct, and create but to perform their narratives in an effort to reimagine and reposit their very corporeal existence in society. Their gaze, both literally and meta-phorically, is fixed in a defiant stance against their designation as the Other. Their body and voice have become their resistance, performing not only the unspeakable tragedies endured but also the empowerment and freedom to create their own future histories. Now, for more than two generations, black women artists have supplanted, deconstructed, and reimagined their own bodies in direct defiance of a constructed fiction. They have revived traumatic histories in order to insert new narratives; protested their objectification and have laid themselves bare to show the depths of their soul's longing and struggles as well as their own alienation. They have found catharsis in embracing their liberated selves and their own ability to transcend the state of subjugation.

THE SKIN I'M IN
Black Women, Color, and Video Art

Andrea Barnwell Brownlee

IN *daily mask* (2004), by Maren Hassinger, a woman in black nondescript clothing sits close to the camera and outlines the perimeter of her face with a black grease pencil. Percussive sounds, reminiscent of African drumming, are the only noises that reverberate from the room. As the woman traces her bone structure, she creates a symmetrical pattern on her eyebrows, chin, and cheeks. Her deliberately grease-stained face soon shares characteristics with an idealized mask. For most of this four-minute piece, the subject—the artist herself—performs directly to the camera. At times, she is situated in front of a three-way mirror that suggests a dressing table. There are brief, whimsical moments, as when she draws on a mustache that recalls eccentric artist Salvador Dalí; however, her unchanging stern expression, augmented by the persistent drumming, alludes to the seriousness of the work's content.

Before long, the skin on her face and neck is covered with a luxurious, shiny black coat. At the end of the piece, she sits before the camera, her eyes closed. Then, under dramatic lighting, she suddenly opens her eyes and smiles, dissolving the stern expression she has maintained throughout. The whites of her eyes and teeth are heightened by the stark contrast of her glistening, artificially altered skin. In the final moments, she scowls at the camera, the drumming gradually quiets down, and the lights fade to black. As the piece concludes, there is no question that it is primarily, and unapologetically, about skin color and all of its complexities.

Several scholarly examinations have focused on how perceptions about skin color have consistently played a profound role in determining the expectations, education, economic status, and social stratification of African Americans.[1] Such studies, as well as anecdotal evidence, which most experience or witness regularly, indicate that skin color persists in being a primary cultural signifier. It is the codifier that prompts people to make initial judgments about others. Likewise, it is the feature that encourages people to be on either the offensive or the defensive about their specific station.

Maren Hassinger, still from *daily mask*, 2004

This examination posits that video art is an ideal medium in which to engage in the multilayered discourse about historic and contemporary receptions, perceptions, and implications of skin color. The topic is frequently conflated with discussions about identity and overshadowed by broader conversations about race. Although colorism is often overlooked, this dialogue is rooted firmly in the assertion that skin color (unlike identity and race) cannot be described as a cultural construction and demands a deliberate discussion of its own. It considers the pointed ways in which artists couple a time-based medium and the process of altering their appearance on-screen as the principal means to investigate this underdiscussed topic. Moreover, using analyses of work by Hassinger, as well as Elizabeth Axtman, Ogechi Chieke, Howardena Pindell, and Xaviera Simmons, as a point of departure, this essay illuminates the tenuous interrelationship of skin color, cultural pride, humor, disguise, and shame. It positions video art, with its connections to performance art, music, literature, cinema, theater, and conceptual art, as an important medium by which to grapple with, unpack, and perform the politics of skin.

Maren Hassinger explained that she created *daily mask* to respond to ways that others were responding to her and to comment on how she frequently felt anonymous. She resented that whites often assume that black people are monolithic. She also reflected on the irony that Pablo Picasso looked to African art, as exemplified in one of his most famous paintings, *Les Demoiselles d'Avignon* (1907).[2] While *daily mask* has specific personal references for Hassinger, it conjures up several generic images as well: soldiers camouflaging themselves before battle, the process of applying cosmetics, and African masquerades. Because of the association between blacking up and a stark, yet dramatic backdrop, *daily mask* is, perhaps, most closely aligned with blackface performance, minstrelsy, and a not-so-distant era that is riddled with shame.

Howardena Pindell, still from *Free, White and 21*, 1980

In *Free, White and 21* (1980), Howardena Pindell, like Hassinger, uses video art to underscore perceptions involving skin color, race, and difference. Pindell created this seminal video after several run-ins in the art world. By the 1970s, she had inured herself to being ignored by the male-dominated art world. Further disappointed by white women artists, she found no refuge within the white feminist agenda. She spoke out when they repeatedly omitted her work from exhibitions and protested when they treated her like a token artist. Their continuing disregard demonstrated clearly that art that engaged race was neither a priority nor an interest.[3] During most of *Free, White and 21*, Pindell, speaking directly into the camera, recounts specific racist incidents, assumptions about race, and misperceptions about skin: When her mother was a child, her babysitter used lye to wash off the supposed dirty color of her skin; in high school, Pindell was not accepted into accelerated courses in order that lesser-qualified white students could enroll; and after applying for more than fifty jobs, she was not hired for a single one of them.

The actions of the blonde woman, in yellow turtleneck and sunglasses, who interrupts Pindell throughout the piece, perhaps best illuminate that issues involving skin color remain unresolved. In her disruptive interludes, the woman dismisses Pindell's claims, concludes that she must be paranoid, and describes the artist as being ungrateful for the so-called help that white women have offered her. The condescension in her voice emphasizes her view of Pindell as other, different, and inherently inferior. The taunting woman is actually Pindell in disguise. In contrast with Hassinger, who blackens up with a grease pencil, Pindell peels off the white mask before the camera. As she reveals her true identity, the complex relationship between skin color and authorship is most apparent. The removal of the white mask suggests three other interrelated topics: a declaration that the skin game is over; an intimation that the blonde subject and Pindell have more in common than previously thought; and an assertion that the subject doing the peeling away is actively involved in dismantling perceptions.

Pindell noted that taking off the white mask had deeply personal references:

> The first thing that comes to mind is removing my white relatives. When Lowery [Stokes Sims] and I traveled to East and West Africa in 1973 I became highly aware of the lightness of my skin. I felt that I was too diluted. It was a very strange sensation. I just wanted to get that whiteness off of me. These feelings lasted for a long time, even after I had returned to the States.[4]

Pindell explained that her fair complexion did not prompt any specific incidents in Africa; however, she perceived—and internalized—

that her skin was too light. Her belief that she was "diluted" suggests that she felt watered down, not pure, and less than black. For her, the removal of the mask was a vital ingredient in a powerful metaphoric cycle, which directly linked fair skin, pain, shame, and the removal of whiteness, to reveal a sense of renewed blackness. Discussions about this frequently referenced video focus on the racism and the disappointments of the feminist art world. The brief segments in which Pindell removes her white mask are equally illuminating and require in-depth examination.[5]

Elizabeth Axtman employs a different strategy to interrogate historical perceptions about skin color in her powerful four-minute video *American Classics* (2005). As the piece begins, the subject—Axtman herself—listens to an offscreen character who advises, "Nothing gives you away faster than slave talk. Never say, 'Is you,' say, 'Are you.'" She replies:

> I don't wanna pass for white. I is white. I don't wanna pass for black neither, 'cause that's me too. Lil miss in between, that's me. Nowhere to go. No place for home. I'm just a mistake.

After her brief response, there is a pause and a clear transition in the video. Next, two different voices—one on-screen and the other off—are in a heated exchange. Axtman, the on-screen subject, asks, "I guess I just wasn't light enough for you, was I, Flipper? You had to eventually go and get yourself a white girl, didn't you?" She continues:

> What I mean is you got a complex about color. You've always had it and I never wanted to believe it until now. Only girls you've ever dated have been light-skinned girls. You and Cyrus. Both of you. Both of you.

A few lines later, she elaborates, with sadness:

> I told you what happened to me when I was growing up. I've explained to you. I poured my heart out and told you how they called me high yellow, yellow bitch, white honky, honky white, white nigger, nigger white, octoroon, quadroon, half-breed, mongrel.

Another break in the video follows her grief-stricken reply.

It may not be apparent in the first interlude that the subject lip-synchs lines that were originally spoken by Halle Berry when she played the title role in Alex Haley's television miniseries *Queen* (1993). In this movie, Queen, the light-skinned daughter of a slave and a slave owner's son, cannot find her place in the post–Civil War world. When

Elizabeth Axtman, still from *American Classics*, 2005

she tries to pass for white, it leads, ultimately, to tremendous heartache and sorrow.

It may not be evident in the second interlude that Axtman lip-synchs the lines of Drew (Lonette McKee) from a heated exchange with her husband, Flipper (Wesley Snipes), in *Jungle Fever* (1991), about the affair he has had with a white woman. It is readily apparent, however, that the characters Axtman assumes fight extraordinary internal and sociocultural battles that center around skin complexion.

Later in *American Classics,* Axtman lip-synchs further pivotal lines spoken by other central, fair-skinned black characters in *Imitation of Life* (1934), its remake (1959), *The Spook Who Sat by the Door* (1973), and *Pinky* (1949). By dubbing what she refers to as "tragic mulatto rants" in mainstream movies, Axtman deliberately singles out the one-dimensional Hollywood-generated protagonists who are preoccupied with having skin that is too fair, consumed by the possibility that others will find out they are black, or unable to sustain romantic relationships as a direct result of their anxieties about their skin color.

American Classics relies on the sound, language, and plight of troubled characters. Axtman does not change the color of her face on-screen by applying a black grease pencil or by removing a mask of white makeup; instead, by reciting the specific lines of characters, she boldly inserts herself into highly charged discussions about skin color. The glow from the television screen reflects on Axtman's face—and especially in her eyes. Lip-synching the lines of principal subjects, reenacting climactic tirades, and imitating the hyperdramatic facial expressions of the respective actors are key components of Axtman's examination. Rather than reenacting the scenes or merely reciting dramatic lines in her own voice, she appears to speak the words on the prerecorded tracks, and, thus, adeptly reveals complex emotions. Lip-synching is more often associated with animated characters, recording artists who aim to achieve a desired effect, and the dubbing of foreign films. By matching her lip movements to another voice, Axtman maintains her appearance and simultaneously adopts the sounds and mannerisms of the angst-ridden characters. Her strategy allows her to assume the plight of the characters as well as mock their deeply rooted anxieties that involve skin.

The daughter of an Afro-Panamanian mother and a German American father, Axtman explains that *American Classics* was inspired in large part by autobiographical experiences. She candidly notes that her work is the "performance of the self."[6] She explains: "It's like being a part of the oppressed and the oppressor at the same time. I only have access to one side of my birthright. The one that is the oppressor and the racist, I do not have access to. But I do want the peace of mind that they, the unwatched, have."[7]

Although Axtman acknowledges her multiracial background, she recognizes that white people will not grant her access to white history, privilege, and culture. In her artist's statement, she explains:

> I am knocking on the door of my white birthright, rockin' Nike Dunks with deep soul and much funk. But I don't look familiar through the peephole, cuz this body is both marked and unmarked. As the daughter of an Afro-Panamanian mother and German American father, I play between representations of both, through performance. Can one be both an Other and another? Black is home. Black is there for me when I roam. My work is informed by the performance of the self. It is an attempt to represent the spectrum of emotions of the African American experience: the close juxtaposition of joy and rage, of comedy and tragedy as well as the periodic lunacy of pressing my face against the window to a party I am not invited to, even though I see my father up in there laughing and dancing all off beat.[8]

By lip-synching the overly dramatic lines originally spoken by biracial characters, which are the focus of *American Classics,* Axtman, on one hand, deliberately jeers the downtrodden characters and, on the other, acknowledges that this complicated cycle is infused with her own experiences. This type of imitation is more than a mere exercise for the artist. She notes: "I am really mocking these characters and putting on the faces of those that do not want to be exposed. There's no hiding for me. I'm not interested in passing. But I ask myself, Am I envious of this or am I proud?"[9] While she acknowledges that the movies from which she lip-synchs were made at different times, and that characters may indeed be modeled after real people, she does not buy into the victim role or think it beneficial to suggest that it is difficult for biracial people to function wholly or successfully in the world. In many ways, through her satirical portrayal in *American Classics,* she sets out to "mirror the ridiculous."[10]

Xaviera Simmons incorporates humor and the ridiculous in *Landscape: Beach (density)* (2005) in order to examine the sociocultural implications of skin. Simmons has garnered widespread attention for her performances, photography, and video works, within which she performs or is featured in blackface and wearing a large Afro wig. In this particular work, the subject—the artist herself—sits down on a towel next to a white woman who is sunbathing. On this picturesque yet uneventful beach, people walk by in the background, a lifeguard chair sits on the mound of sand, and waves ebb and flow. The sky is partially overcast, and the whirring sound of an airplane is the only noise.

The principal action of this eleven-minute piece is Simmons applying tanning lotion and transforming her appearance on camera. Unlike regular tanning lotion, Simmons's goes on black. Sitting down, she covers her legs, torso, neck, and then her face. She applies the blackening lotion generously; before long, her entire body is completely covered in an artificial coat of black. At one point, she stands and continues rubbing in the

Xaviera Simmons, still from *Landscape: Beach (density)*, 2005

Ogechi Chieke, still from *Thee Cakewalk Everlasting*, 2006

lotion. The sunbather beside her is moving, yet oblivious to Simmons's makeover. Near the end of the piece, she puts on an Afro wig, adjusts it, and continues enjoying the sun. Although she is on a public beach, no one notices her exaggerated and altered appearance. Eventually, the video fades to black.

Simmons acknowledges the sordid history, humor, desperation, and shame that surround blackface performance.[11] At the same time, she is compelled by the romantic sentiments associated with it, as well as the widespread interest in such black memorabilia as Aunt Jemima cookie jars and Sambo piggy banks.[12] The differing reactions by African Americans to blackface performances in the twenty-first century are complicated. Although some consider them nostalgic reminders of a practice in the not-so-distant past, others want to either disassociate themselves entirely or surround themselves with more celebratory representations of the black figure.

Simmons, an artist who has studied acting, describes her own interest in blackface performance as neither favorable nor unfavorable but, rather, in tune with her ongoing examination of idyllic landscapes, historical romantic environments, and exotic settings. She explains: "I am primarily interested in how to conjure emotion in my work. My work is entrenched in the theater of play, whereby I examine how people can transform spaces into entirely different places."[13]

In *Thee Cakewalk Everlasting* (2006), artist Ogechi Chieke juxtaposes historical footage of black dancers performing the cakewalk against contemporary subjects performing on a runway. *Thee Cakewalk Everlasting* began as a private joke, she explains, when she used performance to examine performance; it evolved into a more serious project that focused especially on blackface performance. She creates her work specifically for an African American audience.[14] Using exaggerated dance movements and pantomiming with two other artists, she performs an over-the-top, unchoreographed series of steps that include scowling directly into the camera and blacking up. The absurdity of the performance is underscored as one of the performers even rubs the grease pencil on her teeth. Chieke noted: "I really wanted to create a visual time capsule. Using time, text, and images, I wanted to consider the lengths and pains to which black people have gone in the process of performing and being seen."[15]

Through her deliberately disjointed performance, Chieke challenges ways that black people have been seen historically and questions how those representations have changed in the twenty-first century. Steeped in sarcasm and an element of counterculture, Chieke implores contemporary performers to consider how, on a regular basis, they participate in and contribute to their own degradation.

Pioneering experiments conducted by Kenneth B. Clark and Mamie P. Clark in the late 1930s and '40s, using black and white dolls, concluded that black children's ideas and attitudes about such basic qualities as good or bad, smart or not so smart, and ugly or pretty were determined by the skin color of the dolls. In 2005, more than sixty-five years later, Kiri Davis, a fifteen-year-old high school student, re-created the Clarks' experiment. Sadly, she achieved the same results.[16]

Because skin-color bias continues and related issues have not been resolved, the works by the artists mentioned herein are even more necessary to illuminate our lives. It is tempting and appropriate to discuss these works under the rubric of performing race—defiance, resignation, frustration, or opposition. However, such discourse does not acknowledge the matrix of fears, trepidation, discomfort, and, perhaps, even

fascination that guides people's perceptions about skin color. The works of the artists discussed here suggest that such concerns are exponentially complex, unresolved, and in desperate need of ongoing dialogue.

Video art—unlike painting, sculpture, photography, and more traditional mediums—requires viewers to allow the work to develop and unfold in order for them to glean the intended meaning. Time-based work, which is inherently linear, equips artists with the tools to create work that evolves from frame to frame. This very potential is what makes video art the optimal medium in which to examine, explore, comment upon, openly resolve, and exploit the ongoing obsession with skin color. There are countless examples of how artists incorporate themselves into their work. Video art, however, which is situated firmly in the intersection of social commentary, autobiographical narrative, performance art, and theater, allows and, perhaps, even encourages the artists to transform themselves before the viewer in an attempt to explore personal concerns that possess much larger sociocultural implications.

In the so-called color-blind twenty-first century, many refuse to believe that skin color is directly associated with privileges and penalties. As colorism and persistent racial discrimination abound, works by Axtman, Chieke, Hassinger, Pindell, and Simmons, among others, which foreground this important topic, are more necessary than ever.

NOTES

1. See, for instance, W. E. B. Du Bois, *Souls of Black Folk* (New York: Oxford University Press, 2007); Anna Julia Cooper, *A Voice from the South/By a Woman of the South* (Xenia, Ohio: Aldine Printing House, 1892); John Hope Franklin, ed., *Color and Race* (Boston: Houghton Mifflin Company, 1968); E. Franklin Frazier, *Black Bourgeoisie: The Rise of a New Middle Class in the United States* (New York: Collier Books, 1962); and Cedric Herring, Verna Keith, and Hayward Derrick Horton, *Skin Deep: How Race and Complexion Matter in the "Color-Blind" Era* (Chicago: University of Illinois Press, 2004).

2. Conversation with the artist, October 10, 2007.

3. See Howardena Pindell, *The Heart of the Question: The Writings and Paintings of Howardena Pindell* (New York: Midmarch Arts Press, 1997), 65.

4. Conversation with the artist, November 10, 2007.

5. Ibid. Pindell also noted that the mask has a permanent smile as she peels it off her face. She explained, "I often have the appearance of calmness when things are bad. When people make racist comments, it's critical for me to have a sense of calm. I do this in order to moderate my outward emotions about race, or when I try to explain what I'm thinking. When I'm in those situations, I can't wear my rage on the edge of my skin."

6. Elizabeth Axtman, artist's statement, 2007.

7. Conversation with the artist, November 10, 2007.

8. Elizabeth Axtman, artist's statement, 2007.

9. Conversation with the artist, November 10, 2007.

10. Ibid.

11. The history of blackface performance has been written about extensively. See John Strausbaugh, *Black Like You: Blackface, Whiteface, Insult & Imitation in American Culture* (New York: Jeremy P. Tarcher/Penguin, 2006); Eric Lott, *Love and Theft: Blackface Minstrelsy and the American Working Class* (New York: Oxford University Press, 1993); and W. T. Llamon, *Raising Cain: Blackface Performance from Jim Crow to Hip Hop* (Cambridge: Harvard University Press, 1998).

12. Conversation with the artist, October 12, 2007.

13. Ibid.

14. Conversation with the artist, October 10, 2007.

15. Ibid.

16. See Kiri Davis, *A Girl Like Me* (New York: Reel Works Teen Film Lab), 2005.

TRANSFORMERS
Video Installation, Space, and the Art of Immersion

Isolde Brielmaier

THE TITLE OF THIS ESSAY playfully references the Marvel comic-strip series *Transformers,* yet it also suggests multiple meanings within the context of the artists and video works presented in *Cinema Remixed & Reloaded: Black Women Artists and the Moving Image Since 1970.* Placing emphasis upon the concept of individuals as active "transformers" and on the process of "transformation," the title refers to artists such as Lauren Kelley, Wangechi Mutu, Adrian Piper, and Berni Searle, who work with video installation. It points to the varied ways in which these artists innovatively use installation to transform physical space, often creating entirely new experiences. The notion of transformers also evokes ideas of electrical transfer and exchange, and, for the purposes of this discussion, refers specifically to the integral and dynamic role that visitors of video installation art play within the work itself.[1] The title also highlights the undeniable ways in which this artform is transformed by the visitor's immersion

Berni Searle, still from *Snow White*, 2001

in the work. Finally, the idea of transformation underscores the experiential aspect of video installation art and the specific format in which artists present work, visitors actively experience it, and, through this exchange, the way that meaning is generated, altered, and continually reinterpreted. The idea of transformers is thus wide-ranging and encompasses the conceit that visitors' engagement and negotiation with the art results in a transformative process, whereby the work, meaning, and role of the visitor continually change, and no aspect of this dynamic remains fixed.

The artists of *Cinema Remixed & Reloaded* demonstrate that video projection and installation expand the capabilities and perceptions of art—the medium of video, in particular, by pushing the perceived boundaries of space and concepts of reception. In many ways, these artists fuse ideas about art, space, presentation, and active spectatorship into one fluid process that is dependent upon—and endlessly changes the definitions of—all four of these elements. Therefore, the artists who utilize this artform

INTERVIEW WITH CAMILLE BILLOPS

Rhea L. Combs

Interview with Camille Billops, *a public program, was held at the Spelman College Museum of Fine Art on October 22, 2007, and was conducted by Rhea L. Combs.*

Rhea L. Combs: I am honored to be here this evening with Camille Billops, a dear friend and colleague. Camille, describe how your career started.

Camille Billops: I'm from Los Angeles. I went to Catholic school there, and was always an artist. I even have one little drawing from fourth grade. That was the beginning of my art or, maybe, some evidence of doing art. I came from a family that didn't have many books. What we did have was a lot of fabric and food. My father was a cook, my mother was a wonderful dressmaker. I hated sewing, but in all of my work I drew these dresses that I didn't make; that was the influence of my mother. I started appreciating this when I was much older, in hindsight, thinking about the creativity of my parents.

My husband asked the same thing about his blue-collar parents, from Oelweim, Iowa: What did they give us? We're now classified as legally old. What did they give us by saying, Go to school, get educated? They didn't care whether we went to university or not. But they did give us something: style. They gave us a way to perceive that we could build on. Now, in our seventies, we're eternally grateful for that.

RC: In what medium did you start?

CB: I had oil paints, but I didn't paint pictures—I painted my bow and arrow set. I had a doll, a little white doll, that I made a nun. I made her a nun after I straightened her hair so much, it came out. I got to play and do things little children do. There's really no one thing; it was just the experiment of my life. I got to express myself. My parents worked as domestics, and they didn't try to make us little bourgeois children; they let us alone. My daddy had his comic books, his funny books. I have an altar to my father now. It's a purple chair that he sat in, and if he wanted it, you had to get out. Under that, he kept his funny books. He was an excellent cook, but he was also an alcoholic. Now, I see myself in them through style, through old pictures, wearing hats like they wore, doing things that they did. I appreciate who I am, and I think they've played a great part in it.

RC: When did you begin with sculpture?

CB: Maybe it was the doll. You have all kinds of artists now doing nonsense. You can make a doll and put it in museums. It's according to who's doing the curating. We all know, don't we, that if somebody blesses it, it's fabulous; if somebody doesn't, it's nothing. What we came up with was a sense of just doing things. There was a time when little children could get on streetcars and not be molested by people. My mother worked in service—what they called "in service" at that time; the war actually allowed her to leave service. She was part of a series called *Rosie the Riveter,* the oral history part, "Women That Worked," and has her own book. She talks about her life. I have become so much like her. Maybe she trained us to remember to tell the stories, because, now, we're the oldest ones in the family. We meet once a year—the Gilmores and the Adamses—in Red Bank, New Jersey, and we're the ones that tell the stories my mother told. I don't know how we ended up with a library. We did it because people weren't documenting black actors and people like that. We said, We'll do it ourselves. But no one trained us as librarians. We did things because no one said we couldn't do them.

RC: When did you start collecting?

CB: In the 1970s. Jim—my husband, Jim Hatch—got a grant, an N.E.A. grant, to start documenting people, because there were no books on black theater.

RC: You've been married forty-seven years?

CB: No, we married in '87. Old hippies, baby—old left wing. Hanging out with the wrong people in Echo Park—with C. Bernard Jackson, who was a mentor to George C. Wolfe. In this choir, there were Mexicans, Russian Jews, black people, and some white people. What did we sing? In the 1960s, we were singing Prokofiev's *Alexander Nevsky,* in Russian. Russian Jews taught us how to sing Russian.

RC: You started collecting around the 1970s?

CB: In the 1970s, but we had been living in Egypt. I'm going to fast-forward through my life in L.A. I went to Catholic high school, majored in academics, then went to City College—what people called "silly college" at that time. I majored in playing cards and going to the races. D was for dandy, and F was for fine. Josie Mae Dotson was my stepsister. She came to live with us because her father had married my mother. Together, we both hated him. Josie Mae Dotson was like my early mentor. She was younger, but she was older. I was a nice little bourgeois girl going to Catholic high school. You know, little flip curls. Then, I met these odd people. I met Jim. I met Clarence Jackson. My political life changed. Everything changed. I got involved in theater. They were going to put me in the lead in a Micki Grant production—then they heard this whisper of a voice. They said, No, she's in the choir. But those experiences were part of the thing that made me who I am today. I studied art at U.S.C. If you graduated from City College with a C average, straight C, you could go to ended up spending $6,000. Jim had taken film courses at the University of Iowa. Jim's son had some experience with a camera—not much—but we went to California and said, Suzanne, we're doing a film. She said, About what? We said, About you. And that's how we did it. We jumped in there, and we were lucky enough to end up with one scene that made the film; otherwise, we just had footage. But it was about her survival and what happened to her. My mother's in it; it shows her life and her fashion shows. Essentially, all of our films are family films.

RC: Did you initially want to create a family film?

CB: No, no—we just wanted to do a film about Suzanne.

RC: [to audience] I find it very interesting, even ironic, that she's an archivist. Her family has been documenting itself for years, it seems—since you were a young child.

CB: Since '56.

RC: The beauty and uniqueness of your work is that you're able to integrate these found pieces of footage. You have the ability to bring in moments that may or may not have been considered unique for the family but make it poignant, that resonate—an aesthetic for your work. We see that in *Finding Christa*.

CB: We shot *Suzanne, Suzanne* in '79. We finished it in '82—on a $20,000 budget. We raised money at a raffle, selling one of my big ceramic pots for $2,500, and auctioned another of my pieces for another $2,500.

RC: Can you talk about *Finding Christa*? When did you give Christa up for adoption?

CB: In 1960, when she was four.

RC: Your family-based films tend to deal with very delicate issues.

CB: It was fairly traditional. I didn't find it attractive to be an unwed mother, and I didn't find any men who wanted to be daddy. I made a mistake, so I went back to the crossroads and corrected it. I was with people who were progressive, who assisted me in making that decision. Remember: She was never with me. I made the decision, and everyone fell apart—as expected. I gave her up, and nobody could deal with it, because we're all so riddled with guilt.

You run into trouble with this film for political reasons. You can give a child up if you're blind, a junkie, a prostitute, whatever, but you can't give it up for being an artist. In a book on the film, Julia Lesage wrote that that decision was usually reserved for white males. I wanted to go on the adventure of my life—I didn't want to be a mother. But when men decide they're going to nest, it's a holy order.

RC: This was the general reaction, but you won a 1992 Sundance?

CB: Yes. We found Christa. There was a phone call: Do you have a daughter named Christa? I went, Oh, Lord, twenty years later. They said, She's having health problems. She wanted to know her background. When she was eighteen, I went to the Children's Home Society, in Los Angeles, and left my letter, but they didn't give her the letter. To make a long story short, she called me, and that was the call I was showing in the film. She said she wanted to come. At the beginning, we have some footage we shot when she came through the door at Newark Airport. Everybody was scared to death. I said, Maybe it's not too late to run. But we did it, and it was fabulous, fabulous. It was like a honeymoon. It was my family. Everybody got redeemed.

She moved to New York, and that's when panic set in: I thought, Oh, oh, she wants me to do rock-a-bye baby. That's when the real thing started happening—the letters, the guilt letters, the slashing birds. She wanted me to turn over *Finding Christa*. I finally said to her, No, that's my film. So, I get a letter: At least you got a film out of the deal. We finally had a wonderful moment when I stopped backing up my guilt. Christa, I said, you don't like me very much, and I'm not too fond of you, but I would love to have an adult relationship with you. She said, I would like to work toward that myself. We started on this other road, which is really pretty sound. No more screaming, slamming phones down, acting like an infant. At that time, she was twenty-four; now, she's fifty-one.

RC: In the beginning, when we hear that voice—

CB: Her voice? That was her voiceover. We were shooting film then.

RC: You shot it on a set.

CB: She came to New York—

RC: Then, she asked you these questions?

CB: Yes, yes.

RC: Were they scripted or ad-libbed?

CB: Jim does the dramatic continuity of the films. We don't write scripts, we write outlines. You can't script something for people who are not actors, because they ain't going to say it the same; you don't know what they're going to say. There was one part where I said, Some people think I gave Christa up for my husband; do you think that? And I thought, Oh, God, she's going to say it. She looked at me, and said, Yeah, that's what you did. I thought, Oh, shit—but we got through it. You had to let that come. You had to accept other people's truths because you jumped out there and did it. That's what made that film. The film went to Sundance and won the Grand Jury Prize, along with *A Brief History of Time*.

RC: You still, typically, don't use actors?

CB: No, because they're all docudramas. We just do it about situations. We get people whose lives are involved. We're working on another film about our lives. It'll be fabulous. You can't get an actor for that.

RC: *KKK Boutique* is a little different from the other family docu-pieces.

CB: This is a film about racism—everybody's racism. That was the premise. We based it loosely on Dante's *Inferno*, and I played Virgil. We had a gift shop where you could buy racist toys; then, in the various scenes, we descend into hell. We have people talking about whether they had any racism or not. They couldn't talk about anybody else's racism—they had to talk about their own. Some people lied, so we put laugh lines under them to punish them for lying. Our friends are all in it—people who are brave enough to admit their racism. Jim and I start out with ours: We don't like anybody on the street with an accent. We tried to get to the essence of this. Were people really threatened? Is that when they did it? It doesn't always operate. It's operating when somebody is threatened, so we're charged up all the time to have this emotion—and it's very detrimental. It gives people high blood pressure and all kinds of diseases, because we're so emotionally charged. I'm not always mad at white people, because then I can take that energy and do a piece of sculpture. But if I'm mad and charged, then I can't do anything but die early. That was the point—trying to save lives—saying, Let's try to understand this—and we did it.

We got a terrible review in the *New York Times*. But I don't think it was us; I think they were bitching George Wolfe because we played it at the Public Theater. We were trying to do all the different hells. We had a ball with this thing.

RC: How long did it take you to shoot?

CB: Not too long—once I got the money.

RC: How was the general reaction? with different audiences, generationally, how has it been received?

CB: It was a horror. It was like they wanted to kill me. The film was racist—the film was this. It was really just so awful.

RC: Was that an anomaly or how things went?

CB: It was, it was. Later, when we showed it, if you had a young audience, it was wonderful; it was a fabulous ride. If you had older people, it was so long. You said, Oh, God, how are we going to get through this? But the young people really love it—and that is a very nice thing to witness. I've shown it many times.

RC: What would you say to young women filmmakers who are trying now to produce films? Do you have any thoughts, advice, perspectives that as a woman you would bring to the table?

CB: Film is about money. That's first. It's not an art form you can do without money. You can paint, you can dance, you can do a lot of things, but you cannot do film without money. And I'm talking about film; I'm not talking about digital or those things that now make it more accessible—where people have their own editing machines.

RC: Because you shot *Suzanne, Suzanne* and *Finding Christa* with 16 mm?

CB: It's all on 16 mm. But we have editors, and they are expensive. Digital is not cheaper, it's faster. If you're going to use labs and deal with the technicians and editors, you're going to pay the same amount of money per week. We paid $1,200 per week. Those are the postproduction prices, so you really have to know about money. If you've only got $500, you do a $500 film. You have to learn how to raise money. People say, I want to invest in your films. I say, there's nothing to invest in; buy a print from me. I have, on the back of the films, Angels. About twenty people bought a $500 print, and they got their name on the film. That was it. I raised money like that.

I sell art to make money for film. Raffles—anything. I'm lucky to be a visual artist; I can make art and say, Would you buy this? But there is no investment: These are educational films, distributed by Third World Newsreel—my distributor since 1982. *Suzanne, Suzanne* was in the New Directors / New Films series at the Museum of Modern Art, New York, and later was an educational film for the Lincoln Center Film Society. All you women out there, all you need is the right stuff. Don't give up. You can still be a player.

RC: I encourage everyone to keep Camille Billops in mind as you continue down the road of art, art history, film, women's studies, because this woman is a ball of energy.

CB: I'm seventy-four. I got two brand-new knees.

RC: Still rides her bike around SoHo. Please—give a hand to Camille Billops.

Note: This interview was edited for space considerations.

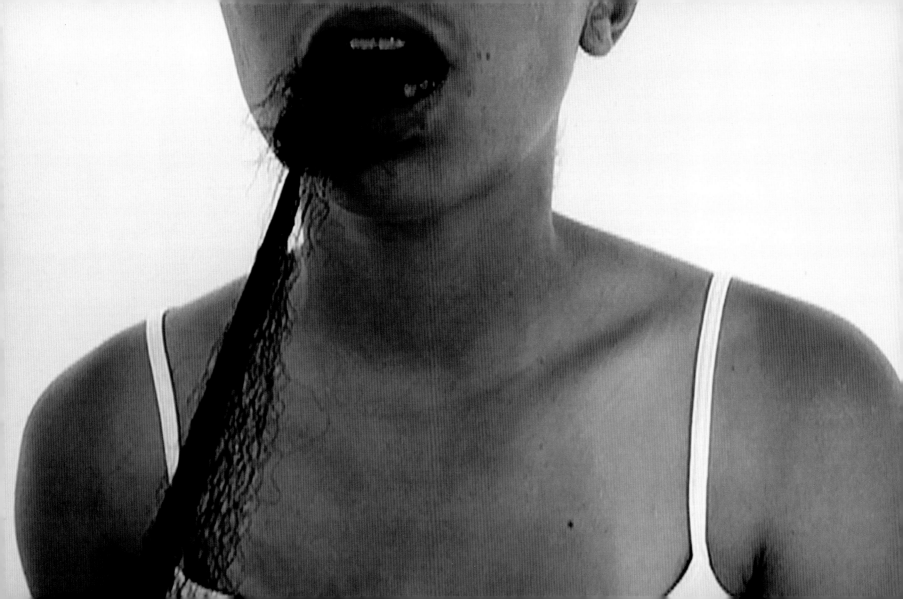

ACE, REPRESENTATION & THE MOVING IMAGE

Valerie Cassel Oliver

Race, Representation & the Moving Image, *a panel discussion moderated by Valerie Cassel Oliver, was held at the Spelman College Museum of Fine Art on September 15, 2007, with artists Debra Edgerton, Jessica Ann Peavy, Pamela Phatsimo Sunstrum, and Lauren Woods.*

Valerie Cassel Oliver: I want to thank Spelman College for supporting this museum and this project. And, of course, I thank my partner in this endeavor, Dr. Andrea Barnwell Brownlee, who does such an exceptional job here. She was very open to walking this journey together. I'm grateful to her and the artists in the exhibition for being the seed of inspiration for this to take place. It is my hope that this event will move from this concept of a panel to that of a conversation, allowing, first, our panelists to engage in conversation and then, like a concentric circle, move outward to you, the audience. We encourage your participation.

Pamela Phatsimo Sunstrum, still from *sometimes I answer,* 2005

First, I want to introduce the women who will be participating on the panel: Pamela Phatsimo Sunstrum, Debra Edgerton, Jessica Ann Peavy, and Lauren Woods. We are also fortunate to have Barbara McCullough seated in the audience. Even though she's not scheduled to participate on this panel, we'll draw her into the conversation as we move forward. Now, a very brief introduction, followed by a series of questions, and then we'll open it up to dialogue.

Prior to the digital age, video was the only artistic medium solely dependent upon technology. Considering its emergence in the late 1960s, the technological advancements have been staggering. For example, we've moved from analog into digital systems in as little as thirty years. What has remained consistent in video art, the things that initially drew artists to it, are its immediacy, its accessibility, and its malleability (the ability to instantly manipulate the content and the form itself). What has also remained consistent in the use of the medium are its abilities to critique and empower. The women in the exhibition have, for two would go and take pictures and narrate them. I was always interested in this kind of storytelling. Fast-forward to college. I went to film school, as well, and always failed my classes, because professors were, like, "Yeah, this is not narrative. Where's the shot or the reverse shot?" They were always suggesting I go to the art department, and I was, like, "What am I going to do with an art degree?" But the first time I saw works by Maya Deren or Kenneth Anger, I realized that there was a context for what I was doing. For a couple of years after school, I was convinced I was going to do Hollywood. I attempted, and it just wasn't fulfilling, so I decided to go to grad school and get an MFA, which was also a difficult transition.

VCO: All of you have touched upon process in discussing your crystalline moments of coming to the medium. So, let's skip forward to talk about presentation. Video and film have contemporarily taken on many forms; both are now so malleable in how they are presented as well. Debra, you touched briefly on presentation in your comments. As viewers move through this exhibition, they will see everything from works on monitors, both single and multichannel works, to projections, to installation work, where sculpture is integrated, to a room of experimental cinematic works. From the panel's comments, it is clear that people are coming into the medium from such different vantage points as film, the visual arts, and even performance. Why don't each of you talk a bit about presentation, and when and where that comes into play in your work.

PPS: The piece that is in this show, I chose to present on two monitors set on pedestals. That was important for me, conceptually. This being my first foray into experimenting with video, I had to figure out what it means to project a piece of video or film versus what it means to experience it on a monitor in a space. I had to think about this once I had my material—how I wanted the viewer to experience it in their body. For me,

the pedestals and monitors seemed to symbolically represent bodies; you confront the pieces as if you are confronting a body. Sometimes, I've shown this piece on taller-than-average-height pedestals so that the mouth in the monitor is at eye level. To suggest to the viewer that they're having an interaction with an actual body was important in this piece. Having to specifically think about how the size of the monitor changes the way the viewer experiences the piece was essential. I've always shown the work on two small monitors. This summer, for the first time, I saw it projected large in a theater, and it was a completely different experience. It really read differently. Conceptually, it became this spectacle—it became a very confrontational piece. There's still something a bit confrontational about it as it is presented here, but I'm fascinated with how the presentation of the work can change the meaning and change your bodily experience.

DE: I started out with video before having an introduction to film—just the opposite, Jessica, of your going from film to video. I do a large portion of my work in video. The presentation always starts with the idea; once I have the idea, I go toward the material and writing the story. The majority of the time when I'm presenting my pieces, they're done as installations. Once I have the idea and shoot the film, I begin to think about the space. It's all very organic, and it's all environmental. Whatever the story, the environment is probably 95 percent of the final work. So, it's the room and the objects that dictate that space, and then the video is an integrated component. The piece that's in here is very concise and to the point. When I originally presented the piece, I projected it on a white kimono, which is the name of the third part of the triptych. I like this present version more than the original, which I felt was heavily weighted toward my mom's story. That is why I wanted the work to be a trilogy. I had done pieces before that dealt with my mom and/or my dad, and that part of me which functioned as a balance between the two. This format is the simplest and goes back to the original idea of being a balanced piece.

JAP: In school, they kept saying things like, "Mix it up, just mix it up." It made me think about how can I change the form—how can I mix things up, or shuffle things, or whatever art term you want to use. But I started to experiment with letting the footage bounce around from one place to another. That's when I got the idea to do things a bit differently. I thought, there are five different women I'm talking about here. Maybe they should all have their own space. Maybe they should intermix with one another and cross into each other's worlds. That's when I started to become interested in the multichannel format, and what you can do with a multichannel situation—what you can accomplish by juxtaposing two images together, and how that can add layers to the work. What I'm working on now continues to be multichannel, using that same idea of mixing up and letting images play off of each other at certain times. But it also allowed me to play with the sound in a way that I really liked as well. When things are single channel, you only have one soundtrack, but with the sound of five monitors, I was able to play off of all five pieces coming at you at the same time. I liked that aspect very much. I was dealing with these five women. If you think about five black women having a conversation, it gets loud—people are talking over each other—so I wanted to capture this cacophony as part of the work, the sound of all five people coming at you at the same time. This was my first time doing multichannel work. It really changed my process a lot. And I'm continuing to work in this way.

LW: I tend to work mostly with projection. Because I started out in film, I'm probably still entranced with projections. Projection is magical; it changes, depending on the space you're projecting in and how large or how small the image becomes. I'm also interested in multichanneled work, and how to flip the traditional way of being an observer and having everything thrown at you. I'm exploring how to make work with projection that references the traditional, yet makes it more interactive still. Projections are less contained; I like that feeling of the spectator being able to immerse themselves in, rather than feel apart from, a work.

VCO: Many of you have alluded to content and how presentation filters into the way the viewer is affected by what you say. Let's segue into content and how the medium is manipulated to evoke a response from the viewer. What's interesting about video art is that it either evokes or demands an active engagement on the part of the viewer, rather than this passive notion of being entertained. The works in this exhibition demand that the viewer think in a way that they wouldn't ordinarily think if they were, say, simply watching a commercial movie. Let's talk about content and some of the issues that have been tackled in the work each of you has presented here or in other work that you've created. In the exhibition, we've touched on a lot of things—issues about empowerment, for example. Lauren, in your work *(S)Port of San Francisco* (2006), there's a sense of desire and longing for the black body that is teased out in the manipulation of the video. The black body, its sum as well as its parts, seems to reverberate in all of the work. Take the issue of hair. Hair is something that we, as black women, are always thinking about. It's a contentious issue born from both legacy and history. Pamela, in your work this hair is in your mouth, and you are pulling out strands, as if you are purging history—literally spitting it out. Let's talk more about content. Who wants to go?

DE: I'll go. I deal with identity. A lot of the work is about memory evoked through storytelling. Recently, I've been dealing with issues of home and how that connects to other subjects. For the most part, I've noticed, more and more arises from this idea of displacement and erasure. When you talk about the idea of the body, the presence of the body, that's a big part of the piece I have featured in this exhibition. It's about absence and presence. The first section of the piece I did in my mom's narrative. The piece was created after her death, so it's the absence of her physical presence, but also the presence of the intangible things she left me, which have become part of my makeup. My dad's narrative was multi-layered. With him, there is a transference of stories, since storytelling is such an important part of his life. There's the aspect of him giving me a story about something in his life that may seem minor but actually had a major impact on the formation of his character. Stories evolve when you pass them on from one person to another, so you hear his voice telling the same story, that I translate and then reveal how it affected me. This same story is then translated back to him. Inside the story, it's about the physical presence of the body—my father as a child—and how his grandfather negated his presence and self-worth. Again, this thing of absence/presence. The negation created for him an erasure, and an absence of something important. That formed how he felt about himself and how he felt about his grandfather. For me, it was trying to deal with the aspects of what was important about two very different cultures, trying to find the similarities and differences—and being resolved to letting go of this constant struggle of how can I make them fit. Maybe they don't fit. It's the realization that there can be differences and similarities and a richness in both these cultures. My parents met in postwar Japan; coming over to the United States, there was this silencing of my mom's culture. My dad, who was sixteen years older, grew up in a time where his culture was silenced. So, I've lived in a household where, even though there were two very rich cultures, both were negated and silenced. A lot of my work is trying to bring back this idea of having a voice.

JAP: A lot of the content of my work comes from whatever I'm thinking about at the time. I tend to switch, sometimes drastically, from project to project. With this particular piece, I was watching a lot of reality television and wanted to shoot the work like a reality program. The characters are speaking directly into the camera and to the audience, very much like a reality show confessional. Traditionally, you're able to say whatever you want and not be judged. But in reality shows, it's the exact opposite. You say whatever, and everyone completely judges you. Think about how the black woman is portrayed on reality shows. Usually, there's only one at a time, and they're often stereotypical: They're either angry or the one that everyone comes to for advice. I was thinking a lot about that at the time. But the work was also created when magazines like *King* and *Smooth* were becoming popular. I started looking through them, and they reminded me a lot of the *Jet* Beauty of the Week. I was, like, "Oh, this is interesting," and I started thinking, "Where have I seen this kind of imagery?" I saw these images when I was a child, and it's progressed to something a lot more . . . what's the word? ["bodacious" from the audience]. It's changed a lot. I started thinking about first seeing these images of women as a child in *Jet*, so a lot of this came about from performance, and having to get a job, and working in a space where everyone was predominantly white, and having to go to work and be this person and then coming home from work and be this other person. It started me thinking a lot about performance—performance in several different ways: performance in life, in general, from situation to situation; performance on television, with reality shows; and the performance of being photographed in these magazines as well. The performance is always trying to be validated by your environment. I was thinking about all of these things. I was also teaching photography, working with some high school students. The kids would go out and photograph the neighborhood. It was a wonderful neighborhood to photograph. I was used to kids coming back with photographs of their neighborhood—just wonderful work. I had a particular group of girls, who, when we uploaded their photographs to the computer, had all taken pictures of themselves. They were posed as if they were being featured in *King* magazine. I was, like, "When did this happen? I'm not a whole generation older than you." When I was in high school, we would never have photographed ourselves that way. So, when did this happen? When did this change occur? Their response to it was, like, "What? That's how we're supposed to be photographed." Because that's all they see. They spend all their time on MySpace and the Internet, and that's how they see themselves. I was, like, wow—that's crazy. Things have changed so much; they don't even know any different. They don't expect themselves to look any other way but like that. Those were the things I was thinking about.

PPS: My work takes a lot of different forms. I definitely think of myself as a multimedia, interdisciplinary artist. But there's always a thread or a spine that connects my practice and the way I think about the content of my work. I was born in Botswana, in southern Africa, but my parents worked in international community development when I was growing up, so my family moved to a different country every two years until I was about eighteen. I've come to understand how I think about my identity in terms of belonging, alienation—what remains, what I see in myself and within myself that cannot be erased. Those residues and traces have become interesting to me. In the piece featured in this show, hair is that residue, that history, that you mentioned, Valerie. It's a source of power in women, the idea of a woman's hair being a source of sensuality, of sexuality, but also a symbol of a dangerous woman, a woman loosed, a woman with uncontrollable hair. In this particular piece, I was interested in the mouth, and how oral history can all be embodied in hair—and also the idea of multiple selves. In the way that I display the piece here, these two monitors create a kind of call and response. In my 2D work and the other work I do, I'm always repeating figures, tracing and retracing a figure over and over, multiplying these bodies in a way that is creating my own community or rewriting my own history. I'm interested in how issues of identity become blurred and how you can think of yourself as never fixed—a self that is always shifting and blurring lines. I'm always interested in how my body is read by others, and how I present, or perform, my body to others. That's central to the way I work.

LW: From project to project, things seem to jump drastically. If I were to identify a common interest, it would be the invisible dynamics, whether it's in looking at a city and how it functions or how people function, interpersonally—those little, bitty, tiny, and minute gestures that reveal something. I work in what I call "ethnofictively." I work in an ethnographic style, but I acknowledge that it's very subjective, it's very much a reflection of who I am. I'm not trying to document some truth and portray it; I tend to go out and watch things and people with my camera. Sometimes, I work in appropriate imagery to try to figure out what there is beyond the narrative or the script. With this particular piece, *(S)Port of San Francisco,* I came upon this little happening at the Port of San Francisco—this dynamic of break-dancers that are there every weekend and the crowd that watches them. I became interested, simply, in where it was, this port. I immediately thought of the auction block and what it meant to have a group of black men performing in this circle, and how people were surrounding them, entranced. Initially, that was my interest, watching how the power dynamics have shifted in this particular situation, and trying to figure out who really had the power and the control. Obviously, it was the dancers. They completely ran that whole dynamic. For four months, I'd go every weekend and just shoot and shoot and shoot and watch people. No one knew I was watching—they just thought I was photographing the dancers—so these little seconds would happen and I'd just be, like, wow. I'd capture it, go home, and then slow it down. I tend to start there; then, I'll aestheticize more and more and more, and I consider that the fictive. That's my own subjectivity, but the more subjective we become, or the more we include ourselves and implicate ourselves, we can touch some sort of ethos—we can touch something about the human condition.

VCO: I love this aspect of voyeurism. Being outside, yet being on the inside, and imparting these moments both as an insider and an outsider and where the two of these converge, as well as when you allow the audience to bring their own perspective to bear in how the work is read.

Let's now have a conversation among ourselves. Pamela, is there something that Lauren has touched upon that resonates in your work? Or, are there questions that you would like to ask each other? When and where do you find your works converging? How do you see yourselves within the overall practice presented in this exhibition? You are the extension of a history, the younger generation in terms of this exhibition. I'd like to drag—I mean, ask—Barbara to pose some questions to the panel. Barbara, you've seen the evolution that's taken place with the medium and how it has been utilized; you've paved a way for many young women to come after you and take on the familiar issues and challenges. How does it feel to see such issues as ritual and masking being discussed now? I'd like to expand the conversation to allow it to become more of that concentric circle I described earlier.

DE: I have a question for all of you. One of the things I did when I realized I was going to be part of this show, since I didn't know everybody or their work, was to go online and Google. I tried to get as much information as possible. I read interviews, and I noticed people talked about their influences and the triggers that may have sparked them into doing what they're doing. So, I've been wondering what kinds of influences each of you've had.

PPS: Actually, a couple of the artists in this show were very influential—Wangechi Mutu's and Berni Searle's work, especially. I did my little dance when I saw the list of artists! I was, like, Oh, my gosh—I'm in a show with these ladies! What excites me about both of these women is that they think about themselves, their work, and their identities in the same way I do. It's often about the slipping place, that place where identity becomes tricky, blurry, and forces the viewer, or the audience, to think and not allow any easy resting places. You're always forced to ask a question, and just when you think you've figured it out, there's another element to the whole equation that upsets everything. I'm passionate about artists who are committed to shaking up what we expect to see, what is traditionally considered acceptable subject matter. I'm really interested in all the postpeople—postcolonial, postfeminist.

LW: My influences, coming from experimental cinema, are people like Maya Deren and her *Meshes of the Afternoon*. The very first work I did—everyone called it experimental, but I didn't know what "experimental" was—everyone said, That's Maya Deren. I was, like, "I don't know who that is." I went to see her work, and I thought, Yeah, that is Maya Deren! Artists like Deren were pretty influential in my work, as well as some Hollywood directors. Spike Lee—I think he's a genius. I like the way he plays with the conventions of Hollywood and turns them around. So,

Maya Deren mixed with Spike Lee mixed with John Rouch, an ethnographer, who did early cinema work all over Africa. Even though Rouch's films are messed up politically, they're interesting. He coined the term and the whole idea of *ethnofiction,* basically acknowledging that an outsider cannot go into a culture and expect to get something real. He would go in and give cameras to his students. He would let them shoot, and then they would create a sort of narrative. It was really a fiction, but at some point it became a document of what was happening at that time. He screened in these remote African towns and villages, first, to get feedback. He was pretty influential. When I came into art and was looking for black women video artists and filmmakers, I read so much, but I didn't have access to any of the material to watch. Slowly, I'm still getting access to these things. Reading about Camille Billops's work—reading about it, even, has been pretty influential as well. And Cheryl Dunye. When I saw the list of women, I thought, Oh, my God, because these are the women that I'm trying to see.

Jessica Ann Peavy, still from *Note to Self: There's a Hot Sauce Stain on My Gucci Bag,* 2006

JAP: I felt a similar thing—I was excited about the show. It has so many people, and the span of artists is amazing. It includes many of the artists I studied in school. It's fantastic. But Adrian Piper, specifically, is someone who has been of interest to me. Particularly the piece *Cornered* (1988), because, again, she's speaking directly to her audience, and I like that. I like that confrontation where you are truly engaging the person who is watching. They're not watching you, but you're addressing them in a way. It's something I'm interested in; it's something I do a lot in my own work. "Blaxploitation" films have always been interesting to me. I grew up watching—probably shouldn't have been watching—*Coffee, Foxy Brown, Sweet Sweetback's Baadasssss Song.* A lot of those films are important and interesting. It's the first time black people are getting to be the directors, have these all-black casts and a lot of control. Yet, there's

a lot of sexuality, a lot of violence, and certainly a lot of people have their reasons for liking or disliking these films. It's great when we can come to a place where we can be happy that there's something with black people out there, where we can have the option to either like it or dislike it. It's a big stepping stone. Not just, "Look there's someone black," but we can actually choose and critique and think about it. That's why those films are so important. They have always been of real interest to me, something I think about a lot—and having these strong female characters that may be too sexualized for some people's taste—but it's there, and we can talk about it. It exists, so let's not pretend it doesn't.

PPS: In regard to black women's bodies, and what we choose to reveal in our work, I've been thinking about this a lot, especially in some of my newer animations, and using my own body in my work. It's a taboo, actually. What, as brown women, do we reveal in our work and in our lives as well? In Debra Willis's work, she talks about the partially clothed black woman as being in a state of undress, our bodies on display. I'm interested in a lot of the work in the show and especially a lot of the work of those sitting at this table. I think we're criticizing the status quo in a way by not allowing ourselves to be limited to the rules of what we choose to reveal. What do you women think about the exoticized brown body, the nude brown body, the naked brown body? What does that mean for all of you in your work? Not as a female, just the body.

DE: I wish I could say I was one of those women who was comfortable with my body. I could be in my own video and display it. But I'm one of the ones that's sitting back going, "Oh, gosh. Is it good enough? How much do I want to display?" An interesting thing happened to me this summer when I was in San Francisco, visiting. I was walking on the street. It was hot, so I was wearing shorts and a tank top, but I didn't think I was wearing anything revealing. This homeless man looks at me, and says, "I need some money, but it looks like you need a boob job." I didn't know how to react—already feeling self-conscious about my body, and then to have somebody on the street, like there was a camera in front of me, and the person was very loud, and there were a lot of people. Inside, I thought, "Am I supposed to react to this? Do I keep moving? How do I respond—besides melting into the pavement?" It just fed into the insecurities I was already having, because of media and society, and always being told how we're supposed to look, and what's supposed to be beautiful. Then, to know that even people on the street are making judgments of total strangers—that person having the boldness to say this. If I had been bold, I would have said, "This is none of your business." Instead, I was a deer caught in headlights. I was so shocked by this comment, I couldn't help thinking: This is my body; it's not out there for display or for you to decide what I'm supposed to be doing with it. So, I straddle this fine line in how I'm affected by the media, because of this whole idea of the body and how they want to describe it, and how we're supposed to decide what is good and bad. It goes back to hair, too. What is good and bad hair? It's all about what we're bombarded with. How we hold on to ourselves and those pieces of ourselves without being affected by what's going on is really hard.

LW: That happens all the time in San Francisco. I've been followed five blocks and someone—a homeless dude—points out every insecurity. For me, its not because I grew up like a tomboy, but my father didn't have any sons, so I think he made me and my sister into a combination of his son. I don't tend to work with my body, or even think about my body, or the female body. My body comes out in my work subliminally. I feel like the combination of the voyeurs and the dancers is my body. I'm not sure if that makes sense. I attempted to work with my body once, and it was difficult; for the first time, I was working with themes specific to female and femininity. It didn't feel right; I couldn't do it. I couldn't joke about it or anything like that. The body appears in my work, but I don't place it there. It appears through all of these other elements.

Barbara McCullough: I'd like to comment. It was interesting listening to the influences all of you have, and how you deal with your image. A long time ago, I did a piece in which I exposed myself—not just who I was in contemporary America but stripping away all of those things to reveal the nappiness of my hair, the roundness of my nose; I transformed myself into what could have been a traditional African woman. What I'm finding interesting with you guys is that you all embody the holistic concept of body, mind, and spirit. Whether you intentionally convey that, it's

Lauren Woods, stills from (S)Port of San Francisco, 2006

there. It's interesting how each of you exposes that. In my own personal work, it was like dealing with experimental cinema or video and the idea that, in the community where I was, the term meant not substantive, not political, but art for art's sake—having very little content that was worthwhile beyond just looking at the piece and passing it on. It didn't have anything to do with the conceit that, as a feminine being, you have the right to express who you are as a female, what your sense of spirituality is, or what your sense of community is. It was very difficult to do the work and get it accepted and viewed as something other than exploitation of the physical form. You know, not just soft porn but, basically, that I can show you who I am and strip away your preconceptions and deal with myself as a being coming from way back when, of generations with traditional backgrounds. And I can take those traditions and put them on the table and put them on the altar and deal with my own sense of spirituality, and how I create the ritual of transition or acceptability for me and my community. You guys are talking about Maya Deren and underground cinema from the 1950s, and Jonas Mekas and Stan Brakhage and

Alejandro Jodorowsky, who did *El Topo,* and the ways of expressing some of what you're saying differently. You guys are talking about the people who influenced you; it was very hard for, let's say, my generation of women artists to figure out who our influences were. So, who were they? They were the people I mentioned. But there were also people like Zora Neale Hurston, Betye Saar, Senga Nengudi, and Shirley Clarke, who was underground and who wound up being my teacher and mentor when I was at UCLA. It was a whole combination of things that influenced you, but you all go back to Maya Deren, and that goes back to the body, mind, spirit. That was what was in her work—dealing with the magic, dealing with the spiritual nature of who we are. Of course, with Zora, it's taking us to our community and finding those influences that made us who we are, that help us to express our affinity for our culture, and putting it out there for other people to see.

VCO: How has the discourse evolved? How much of this dialogue has shifted over time, Barbara? What has changed and what remains consistent? This is a reexamination of what was happening in the 1970s, particularly among women. There are many exhibitions that are out now, such as *WACK! Art and the Feminist Revolution* and *Global Feminisms,* that are examining how women artists have used artistic media to explore issues that impact and influence them, and the ways in which they've deconstructed what has, historically, been a male-dominated medium. Certainly, film and video was, at the time, a very male-dominated medium. How have people deconstructed that, and how have generations been influenced, and how has that reverberated over a period of thirty-five years? What does it mean when we are still talking about issues of the body? What does it mean when we're still talking about issues of hair? What has shifted? What has evolved? Is it a spiral or is it just a circle?

BM: I think it's both the spiral and the circle. More of you are now discussing this in an open forum. Because of what we see, because of what's on TV, because of what the media shows us, because of what we see in music videos, because of the images we see that are so negative—that are not necessarily true depictions of who we are—it's important that the work you do is out there so that there is another side. What's happened is that the media has denigrated us far beyond where we were decades ago. That you're doing the work and showing it, whether it's personal and from your family or observing other people and showing how they view things, it's all-important that you continue doing this, because, as I said, a long time ago I only knew one other woman who was dealing with video art. Everybody else was more documentary. My thing was so subjective. It's not really an objective observation or depiction of something; it's all sent through the filter of who you are. That you are not afraid to let it go through your subjective filter is something people need to see. Maybe this is why it's coming back, because there's still this negative depiction of us, and it's gotten worse. To dig away at that and

Barbara McCullough, still from *Water Ritual #1: An Urban Rite of Purification,* 1979

strip away at that, to give another point of view and another perspective, is important.

VCO: I cannot overemphasize how groundbreaking this exhibition is in bringing together generations of women who have used the moving image—and to collectively offer this work to the public. In organizing this exhibition, we, Andrea and I, found the arena so expansive that it could not be done in one part. So, there are two parts to this exhibition. And, with this, we are just scratching the surface. Women are taking on the medium, critiquing it and deconstructing what we see every day. The concept of taking something that is so familiar and accessible as the moving image, is the thing that draws us in. Now, more than ever, people are fixated on the moving image. Reality TV shows have replaced the fiction of the soap opera. Suddenly, Hollywood is bringing "reality" to us. In a way, it's very subversive and detrimental, because people understand reality TV as that—reality. It doesn't allow a lot of room for fiction or for people to create their own reality. Instead, they rely on their television sets.

I'd like now to open the discussion to our audience. Thank you for being engaged and patient. I now want to hear from you. Do you have questions for the artists? Barbara, why don't you just pull up a chair? I'm sure that people are going to have questions for you.

Audience member: My name is Myron and my question is for Jessica Ann Peavy. I am a photographer. I remember a while back seeing a similar project done by a professor, whose project was to give cameras to children to photograph their neighborhood. Then, they'd compile it and make a collage. The subject matter was mostly of their surroundings. When you say that the children in your class photographed themselves "that way," what, specifically, were you referring to?

JAP: Mostly, they were hypersexualized images of themselves. I wasn't reprimanding them, I just wanted to have a conversation about why they felt they had to represent themselves that way. They all said, "Well, how else would we photograph ourselves? And, can we put it on MySpace when we're done?" I was just, kind of, like, What? It never dawned on me that that's what they wanted to do. I had never had that experience before. This was early 2006, when MySpace was a new phenomenon. If anyone else on the panel wants to comment on this, please do. I'm interested in how people between the ages of fourteen and forty spend the majority of their time on the Internet. This is now even beyond cinema and television—people are not looking at that anymore—people are spending all day on the computer. How is that going to change the discussion of media, as well as race and media, and having the ability to move quickly? Filmmakers and artists do not necessarily have to wait for that deal, or

for that curator to call you; you just go to YouTube and everybody sees it. We have more control. It's more democratic. Everybody can put whatever they want on the Internet. You don't have to be involved in Hollywood anymore. These videos are getting thousands and thousands of hits by so many different kinds of people. That's definitely going to change a lot about how we think of media.

Audience member: My name is Marcia Jones. I'm a professor of art at Clark Atlanta University, and I have a couple questions. The first deals with how your work is so subjective, and how the formalist construct is still concerned with the subjective story, and how it holds this at arm's length from the viewer, denying them accessibility: Do you find that this subjective space is actually the most vulnerable space? It's not arrogance that's holding this at arm's length—it's your own resistance to accepting my subjective story, not me telling it. Now, I'm still detoxing off of graduate school. I heard things like, "It's so much about your arrogance. And if it's not accessible to the people, what are you saying?" But I'm telling my story, and my story is very accessible to pretty much every woman, if you pay attention. But what you're showing me is that this arm's length is really from you to me, not me to you. Do you all find this to be the case from viewers?

LW: I like to work in communities; there's definitely a conflict working with art with a capital *A*. After you leave art school, after you leave the gallery system and try to put it out to the public, you have to deal with the public having a different language that's not the same language you're speaking in this particular world. In that sense, it's the same thing. There's this misunderstanding that seems like arrogance, when, really, it's insecurity—and it's masked very, very well. My balance is in trying to find as many venues for the work—not just staying in the museums stance, because it's an alternative from mainstream media. No matter how someone chooses to tell their story, in this kind of environment you're telling your story in a different way, and that may not be as toxic as television or mainstream Hollywood or whatever. The actual act of making, no matter how it gets out, is the goal. Being able to do that, being able to impart or pass on to others who are younger than me that you don't have to go this route, you don't have to go this commercial way, for me that's the thing.

DE: In our patriarchal society, sometimes I feel that as a black woman we have the smallest voice. Just being able to do the process and say to ourselves, Look, I've got a voice and this is the medium I'm choosing to use, and there are people coming in and viewing it, and they understand it or they accept it. I feel that it empowers me to say that I'm speaking and, maybe, some people out there are listening.

JAP: This is the perfect opportunity to bring the Internet conversation back into play. Everyone has the power to create media in some way and put it out there. If you don't like what's on television, you can create something else; that's what's great about it. What's lacking is a balance of things on television. There's nothing to offset *Hot Ghetto Life* on BET; there's nothing else. It all starts with my students, who are the next generation of people to come up. They're already invested in so much stuff on commercial television.

VCO: Audiences are the last to know just how complex their own culture can be, because there's a constant desire to simplify and flatten it so it's palatable for consumption. To respond to reality TV, to say, "No, this is not my reality—*this* is my reality," is a point well taken, Jessica. It's something we'll explore in part two of the exhibition, because there are several artists who are using video for Internet screening and only for web viewing.

Audience member: My name is Uri Vaknin, and I am a gallerist. First, I'd like to say that this show is more than groundbreaking; it's a seminal moment in American art history. I've been showing video art for years. I opened my first gallery with a Bruce Nauman video from the 1960s. As a gallerist, it's always been very difficult to show video art, because the consumer doesn't buy it. There's a perception of a lack of preciousness, unless it's presented in a sculptural or installation situation. The only time I've ever been able to sell video is Tony Ousler's work, because it is sculptural. As an artist, it's great to be in a museum exhibition, especially the Whitney, or whatever it may be. But there's a moment in an artist's career when they receive a check. There's such validation to that; it makes you want to create more and it helps you create more. Not just in day-to-day eating, but it makes your mind more creative—because that's the way that value is placed on certain things. You, Jessica, talked about putting it out on YouTube and the Internet. How do you do it, in your personal experiences, having gotten paid by a consumer—and I'm using the word "consumer" rather than art collector—who says, "I want to buy that piece of video"? Do you copyright it? I'm totally changing the tenor of this because, obviously, I'm a gallerist, but also because my number one goal is getting artists' work out there. How do you do it? Unfortunately, not everyone is going to come down to see this exhibition at the Spelman Museum, so my question to all of you is, Are you copyrighting? Do you think about these things when you do the work? Putting it on YouTube is fantastic, but unless you're trying to be a singer and give a snippet of who you are, if you put your video out there, you've almost sold your soul in a way. To me, this is a very important topic.

BM: For me, income may come once a year, and it may be very small. A good year may not be too bad, but it's never been big. That's the way that is. But it's gratifying if the work's going to a university, because there're going to be students affected by what they see. That's my goal: to effect change on an individual level, because I come from an era where mass change was thought about and, in certain instances, did what it did. If you can effect change on a very individual level—and schools taking and running a piece of my work, that's icing on the cake—it doesn't have to be a lot of money.

VCO: With video, especially projections, there has been a strong push to create a retail template. Generally, the work gets sold as an edition. Video as projection work has come into the market in a way, very different from film. It is a very interesting question. Have any of you sold work beyond Barbara?

JAP: I've only sold stills. I have not sold videos. I do make stills of all of my work. That's the only way for me to sell work, not having a gallery or someone to push the work at this point.

LW: Since I'm a filmmaker working in art, already I'm in many different worlds—or on the outside of many worlds—so I learned, for lack of a better word, a hustle. My painter friends have learned that this is the direction they have to go. But, for me, different types of work fit in different situations. I have work that I sell in galleries, and I make editions and sign them. More or less, people are paying for the signature and the special box it comes in. Because you can dupe it, anyone can bootleg anything. But I also have the single-channel work that goes through distribution; it's more geared toward festivals. Then, I have the public work that I try to get grant money for, and I find the process that way.

That first experience of receiving a check for a DVD I burned off of my computer was crazy. I don't know how the gallerist decided to sell it or got the people to buy it, because I think it was the first video in their collection. It was very inspiring. I'm always envious of painter friends, because I sometimes wish I could dedicate myself fully to this and be able to support myself from it.

Uri Vaknin: Photographers used to say the same thing. It used to be that you didn't understand the preciousness of the photographic image. But, now, it's like fashion photography—everyone wants to own it. I want to make sure that video is going down that path—and how it can go down that path, whether it's through copyright or protection. The sculptural video has always been able to accomplish that.

DE: I'd like to turn that question back to you, because you say you represent video artists. How do you approach this idea of being able to sell video work? We had that conversation last night, and I mentioned to you that I gave a copy of one of my pieces to a friend, and my friend emailed me back and said, "I've been showing your piece all around, and I have a couple of friends who would like to burn copies of it." I was, like, Huh? Because I had given it as a gift, and there was not a validation that this is a piece of artwork I've given you. I related it to, "Well, if I gave you one of my paintings, would you Xerox it so that your friends could have it?" They equate it to Blockbuster Video and see it as something that can be reproduced. That's what made me think, God, maybe I should be copyrighting this stuff, because I don't have any clue if I were to give it as a gift, what's going to happen. I'm not even sure what the answer is.

LW: I think it's just the thing that surrounds it. Video is such a democratic medium, it can't be contained in the same way. People who support video artists are doing it for the act of supporting them—supporting this artist. They probably say, "We know we can bootleg it from somebody else, but we're supporting it because we like what you're doing." People want to be patrons in that manner, rather than being patrons in the sense of owning an object.

VCO: Video art is just that—it's art. You can create editions very much the same way that printmakers or photographers make editions. You can copyright it. And if people pay money for it, they're not going to burn a copy of it to give to someone else, because, ultimately, it devalues the work. I would encourage each of you to think about this, because you don't want to sell yourself short. You can, in fact, earn a living from your medium of choice. Don't think so quickly that it's a democratic medium and I can't earn a living off of it. I know that we live in a different time and that the medium affects your work and that the same arguments and struggles that are occurring in the music industry can also be applied here, but there is a big difference. You are not a commercial industry, you are engaged in commerce. You can control the market and how your work is sold and collected.

Audience member: My question has shifted as the conversation has continued. But I'm on the same page as Lauren. I'm an art advisor. My name is Karen Comer Lowe. I talk to people and help people build collections. Most of my clients are African American; when you introduce the idea of video, there's a conversation about video, but it's a hard sell. Part of that is because it is a democratic medium. Even if you have the works editioned and market them in that way, what stops someone from burning it?

VCO: The fact that they would essentially depreciate the value of something that they've just spent a lot of money to collect.

LW: But when it ends up in a video library, someone like me goes to that video library, and says, "Let's go put this on my computer." I don't necessarily try to show it, but it's there for my own educational experience.

VCO: It would literally depreciate the value of the work. If someone spends $2,000 for a DVD, why would they depreciate the value of it?

Karen Comer Lowe: I understand that from the professional aspect. But just the nature of people, and what we do. You know what I'm saying? We burn CDs. We share music. I have this beautiful artistic video, and it's cool. I want to share it. I want my friends to have it. I paid for it, so why can't I share it—the idea of it? With all of that said, I want to backtrack to my original question. Do you create the video and think of it as something to be collectible, that you want collected? Do you make it with the idea that you want to sell this? Is that why you do it?

DE: When I got into video and installation, my first thought was, Nobody's gonna buy this. What drew me to it is the idea of the added environment and the added motion to the artwork itself. I know it sounds kind of sappy, but the passion of the work is the most important thing to me. Because I am a painter and because I do work in photography, and I do teach, I know that if I need to make money, I have other avenues. When I work with video, it didn't occur to me, until I started hearing other people, like Lauren, say that she'd sold a piece. I was, like, Oh, you sold a piece. Oh, I can sell this? That's when it was, like, Oh, it's an idea. But that wasn't what led me to the medium.

VCO: Dr. Farrington, you had a question?

Lisa E. Farrington: Yes. I think it's a question. What I kept thinking about as you were talking was an article from the 1930s by Walter Benjamin, "The Work of Art in the Age of Reproduction," and the subsequent art movements or, even, artists. For example, Elizabeth Catlett, who worked for so many years in the Peoples' Graphic Workshop in Mexico, deliberately to take the preciousness away from the art and make it readily accessible to the people whom she felt could benefit the most. The work of art wasn't meant to be precious, but something for everyone. There is a paradox here between our individual need to earn a living—I don't think any artist goes into art for that reason—and the benefit, ultimately—and I think all of you, all five of you, are in this place—of teaching and pulling culture forward with you, being able to change the idea that women have this teeny, tiny voice. That reminds me of another book—*The Incredible Shrinking Black Woman,* or something like that. I forget who wrote it. But it's true: All of these students that are making sexualized pictures of themselves are basically copying someone else's idea of what the black woman is. Your goal—at least, I'm hearing this from almost everything each of you has said—is to change that. You're trying to tell the world who we are in an autobiographical voice—which is such a valid voice, and shouldn't be denied—and to raise culture up. If you make some money doing that, great. But that comes first, and then the money will follow. Trying to create work that only people with $2,000 can access seems to go against the essential goal of your self-expression. I'm proud to have the chance to know you. I cannot tell you how impressed I am by this show. I just thought you should know.

VCO: We have time for a quick response, or maybe one last question.

Audience member: I haven't had a chance to look at the entire exhibit yet, and I haven't seen any of your other work, but do all of you, as black women artists, only make art about black women? Why do you think it's important to focus on that?

PPS: I make work about myself. That's always the place it has to start. It has to start with me. I don't think about my work dogmatically, as this is work about being a black woman—it's work about being me. That becomes political, in that it denies pigeonholes, it denies assumptions, it denies stereotypes, and it allows me the freedom of possibility and of operating from a place of pure honesty.

JAP: I'm always reminded I'm a black girl. In every space that I exist it's always this way. If I'm at work or even with my kids, who are mostly black and Latino, the discussions with them are always about that, because it's just how it is, how you exist in the world. Especially in Harlem right now, which is changing so drastically, it's constantly a discussion. For me, it's hard to avoid.

MJ: I'm finding that it's often a kind of safety net, the fact that you're articulating for yourself. It allows a quick escape for the viewer—depending on who the viewer is—to put it there and say, "Oh, it's a black women's issue." Sometimes, this is not about being black—it's about being an artist, first, and about being a woman, too. It's dangerous right now for women to stand up for themselves. It seems like that MySpace culture and mass media has to say something articulate, even if it's "No, fuck you." To say that right now is, like, "She's got some issues." No—it's just that I'm not going to lie down and let you walk on me. It doesn't make me angry, it makes me proud of myself, and that makes me okay with me. It's interesting how this whole thing is shifting. It doesn't have to be just about being a black woman.

LW: I don't think my work is specifically about black women but how artists reflect themselves in their work. So, I am a black woman. Even though the imagery isn't of black women, if you're a black woman and you speak this language, you'll be able to translate certain things—and other people who speak film languages will be able to translate things that other people won't.

LEF: It's interesting. If white men make work about white men, nobody says anything. People make art about themselves.

BM: I've created this piece that is an exploration into why people have some component of ritual in their work. I'm interested in exposing the work of culture bearers—whether or not they're known as culture bearers by other people—because they've made contributions to our society and people need to know about them—people need to hear their voice, how they do their work, and how they influence people, and the relationship of their work to other culture bearers.

LW: Valerie, I want to say thank you to both you and Andrea Barnwell Brownlee. Oftentimes, with exhibitions, no one really talks about the exhibition and the subtleties that happen between paint and everything else. I really feel that this is a room of our own, as Virginia Woolf liked to say. Every detail—even in the choice of the color of the exhibition—this could have been white gallery space, it could have been a traditional black box, but blue, to me, is very significant. When I think of blue, I tie it to other kinds of spiritual realms. All the way around—the work and the space—I feel like it's holistic.

VCO: Thank you, Lauren. I want to thank our panelists for your voice, for your honesty, and your insights. Also, a big thank you, audience, for being here. We encourage you to come back—early and often. There's a wonderful slate of programs being presented throughout the run of this exhibition and we encourage you to support those. Again, kudos to Spelman. And Andrea, my very dear friend, thank you. I'm very happy to be here and honored that, together, we were able to manifest this project.

PLATES

Ina Diane Archer | *1/16th of 100%?!* | 1993–96
Video, color and black and white, sound, 20:00 minute loop

Elizabeth Axtman | *American Classics* | 2005
Digital video, color, sound, 4:00 minute loop

Elizabeth Axtman | *Expletives Owed* | 2007
Digital video, color, sound, 17 second loop

Camille Billops | *Older Women and Love* | 1987
16mm film, color, sound, transferred to DVD, 26:00 minutes

Carroll Parrott Blue | *Dawn at My Back:*
Memoir of a Black Texas Upbringing | 2004
Interactive DVD-ROM

María Magdalena Campos-Pons | *History of a People Who Were Not Heroes: A Town Portrait* | 1994
Mixed-media installation with 3-channel video and sound
Installation, Spelman College Museum of Fine Art (2008)

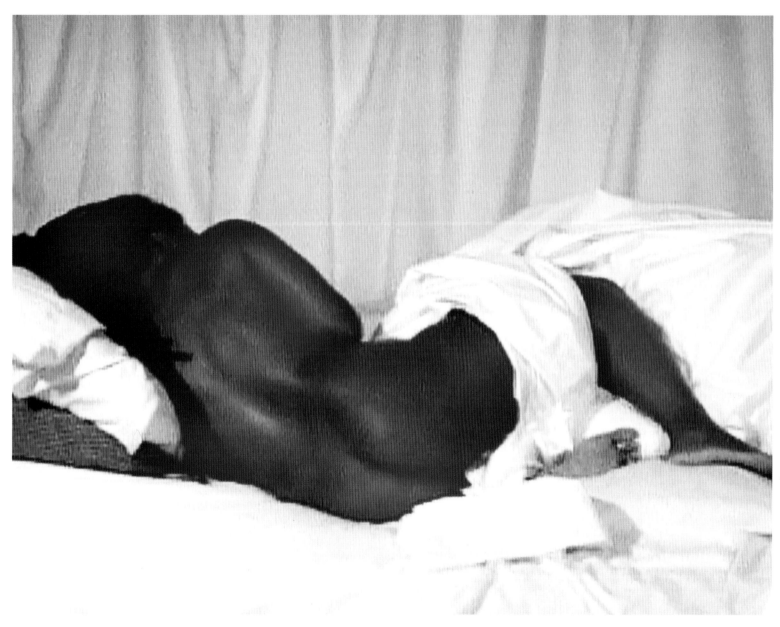

Zoë Charlton | *Dead White Men* | 2005
Digital video, black and white, 1:58 minute loop

Ayoka Chenzira | *Hair Piece: A Film for Nappyheaded People* | 1985
16mm film, color, sound, transferred to DVD, 10:00 minutes

Ogechi Chieke | *Thee Cakewalk Everlasting* | 2006
Digital video, color, sound, 1:31 minute loop

Julie Dash | *Four Women* | 1975
16mm film, color, sound, transferred to DVD, 4:00 minutes

Zeinabu irene Davis | *Mother of the River* | 1995
16mm film, black and white, sound, transferred to DVD, 28:00 minutes

Stephanie Dinkins | *Configured to Infinity, Reconfigure. Stop.* | 2000
Mixed media with video and sound
Above: video stills
Right: detail of installation

Cheryl Dunye | *Greetings from Africa* | 1994
16mm film, color, sound, transferred to DVD, 8:00 minutes

Debra Edgerton | *Retelling Tales* | 2003
Video projection, DVD, color, sound, 6:45 minute loop

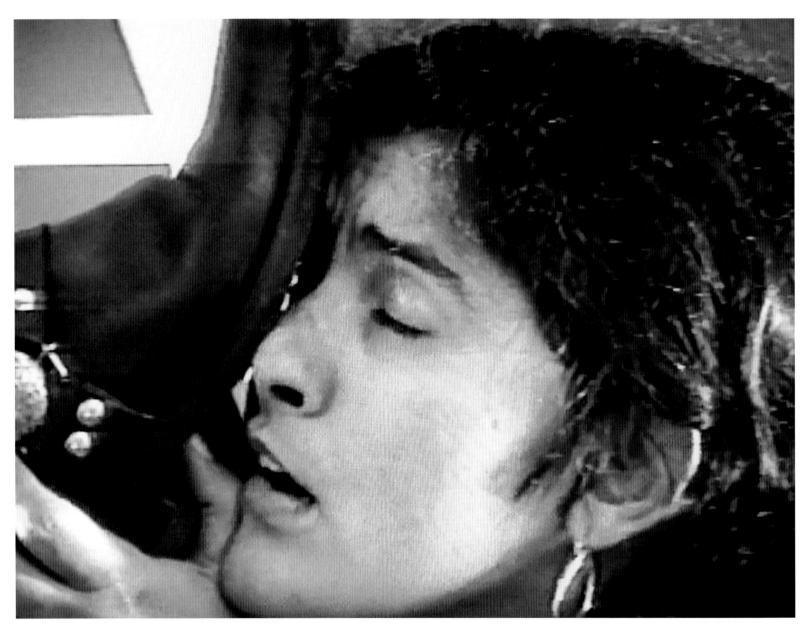

Shari Frilot | *What Is a Line?* | 1994
Video, color, sound, 9:50 minutes

Colette Gaiter (in collaboration with Jeanine Mellinger) | *All Power* | 2008
Interactive DVD-ROM

Leah Gilliam | *Sapphire and the Slave Girl* | 1995
Video, black and white, sound, transferred to DVD, 17:30 minutes

BARCELONA

WIEN

LISBOA

LOS ANGELES

SAO PAULO

Renée Green | *FAM Trailer (Berlin)* | 2007
Digital video, color, sound, 14:00 minute loop

Marguerite Harris | *Flowers & Leaves 2* | 2001
16mm film projection, black and white transferred to DVD, 1:33 minute loop

Maren Hassinger | *daily mask* | 2004
Digital video, color, sound, 3:32 minute loop

Pamela L. Jennings | *Speaks Volumes* | 2008
MAX/MSP software patch with video and sound

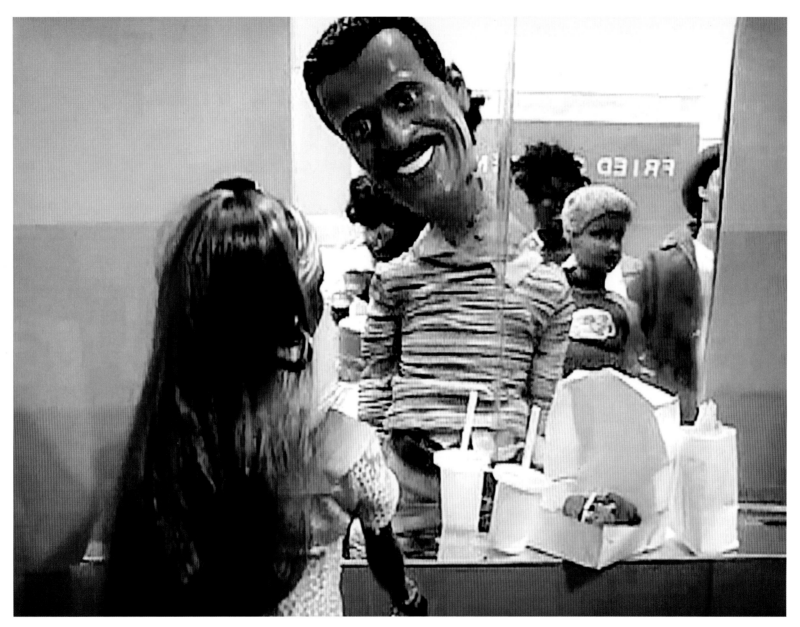

Lauren Kelley | *Big Gurl* | 2006
Digital video projection, color, animation, sound, 8:12 minute loop

Yvette Mattern | *The Zanzibar Project* | 1998
Video projection, color, sound, 12:00 minute loop

Bradley McCallum & Jacqueline Tarry | *Cut* | 2006
Digital video, color, sound, 4:00 minute loop

Barbara McCullough | *Water Ritual #1: An Urban Rite of Purification* | 1979
16mm film, black and white, sound, transferred to DVD, 4:00 minutes

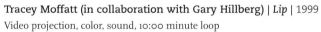

Tracey Moffatt (in collaboration with Gary Hillberg) | *Lip* | 1999
Video projection, color, sound, 10:00 minute loop

Wangechi Mutu | *Amazing Grace* | 2005
Digital video projection, color, sound, 6:29 minute loop

Wangechi Mutu | *Cutting* | 2004
Digital video projection, color, sound, 5:44 minute loop

Senga Nengudi | *The Threader* | 2007
Digital video, color, sound, 11:22 minute loop

Michelle Denise Parkerson | *Stormé: The Lady of the Jewel Box* | 1987
16mm film, color and black and white, sound, transferred to DVD, 21:00 minutes

Jessica Ann Peavy | *Note to Self: There's a Hot Sauce Stain on My Gucci Bag* | 2006
5-channel video installation with sound, 1:52 minute loop, each channel
Above: channel 5 detail; Right: channel 3 detail

Howardena Pindell | *Free, White and 21* | 1980
Video, color, sound, transferred to DVD on monitor, 12:15 minute loop

Adrian Piper | *Cornered* | 1988
Video installation with birth certificates, monitor, table, and chairs
Installation, Museum of Contemporary Art, Chicago

Tracey Rose | *The Wailers* | 2004
Digital video projection, color, 6:19 minute loop

Eve Sandler | *The Wash: A Cleaning Story* | 1999
Super 8 film, color, sound, 9:00 minutes

Berni Searle | *Snow White* | 2001
Dual video projection with sound, DVD format, shot on DVCAM, 9:24 minute loop
Above: frontal view; Right: aerial view

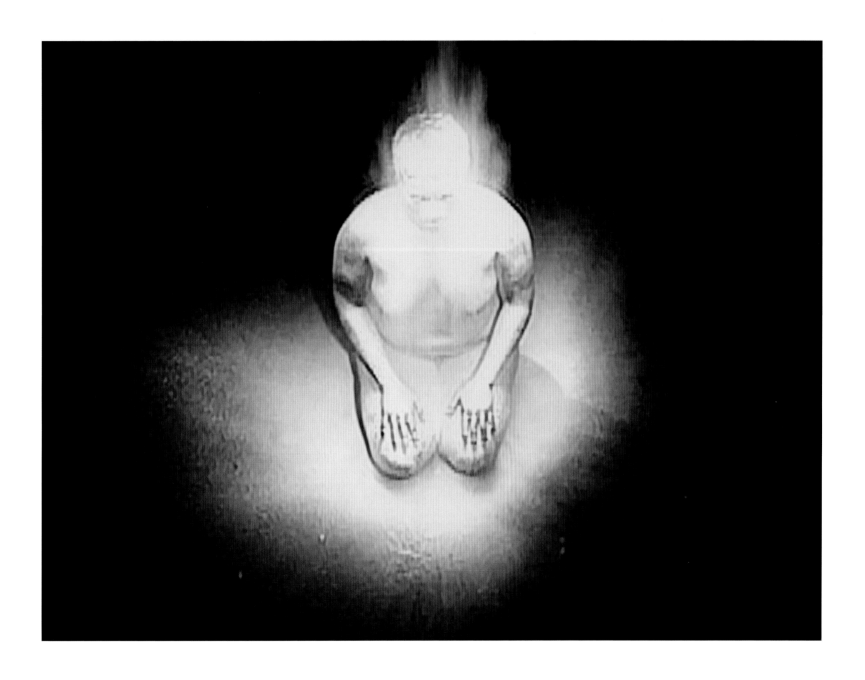

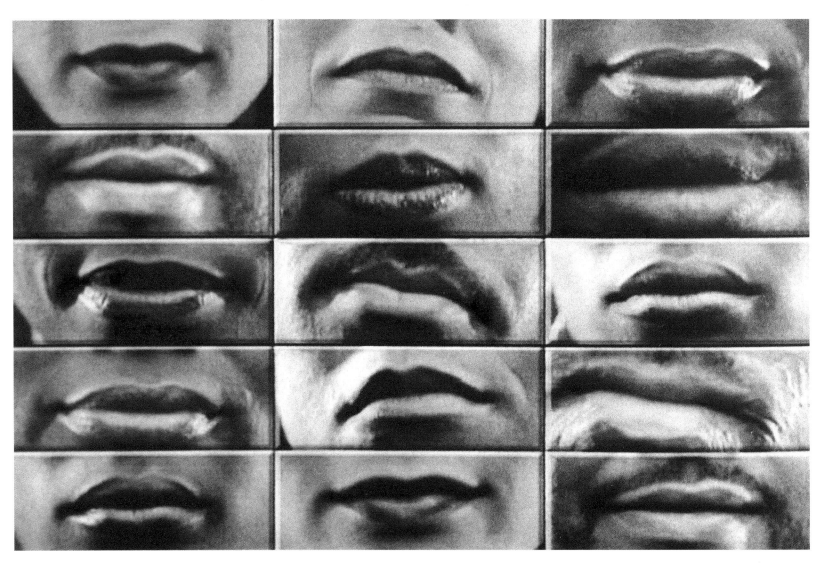

Lorna Simpson | *Easy to Remember* | 2001
Video projection, 16mm film, black and white, sound, transferred to DVD, 2:35 minute loop

Cauleen Smith | *The Changing Same* | 1998–2001
Digital video, color, sound, 5:30 minutes

Pamela Phatsimo Sunstrum | *sometimes I answer* | 2005
Digital photo animation, color, on two monitors, 1:36 minute loop

Jocelyn Taylor | *Armide 2000* | 2000
Video, color, sound, 7:00 minute loop

Kara Walker | *8 Possible Beginnings or: The Creation of African-America, a Moving Picture by Kara E. Walker* | 2005
Video projection, 16mm film, black and white, sound, transferred to DVD, 15:57 minute loop

Kara Walker | *Testimony: Narrative of a Negress Burdened by Good Intentions* | 2004
Video projection, 16mm film, black and white, sound, transferred to DVD, 8:49 minute loop

Carrie Mae Weems | *Italian Dreams* | 2006
Video, color, sound, 10:35 minute loop

Yvonne Welbon | *Monique* | 1991
16mm film, color, sound, transferred to DVD, 3:00 minutes

Paula Wilson | *Turf* | 2005
Oil, woodblock, watercolor, and silica flat on paper and canvas, with video projection
Installation, Spelman College Museum of Fine Art (2007)

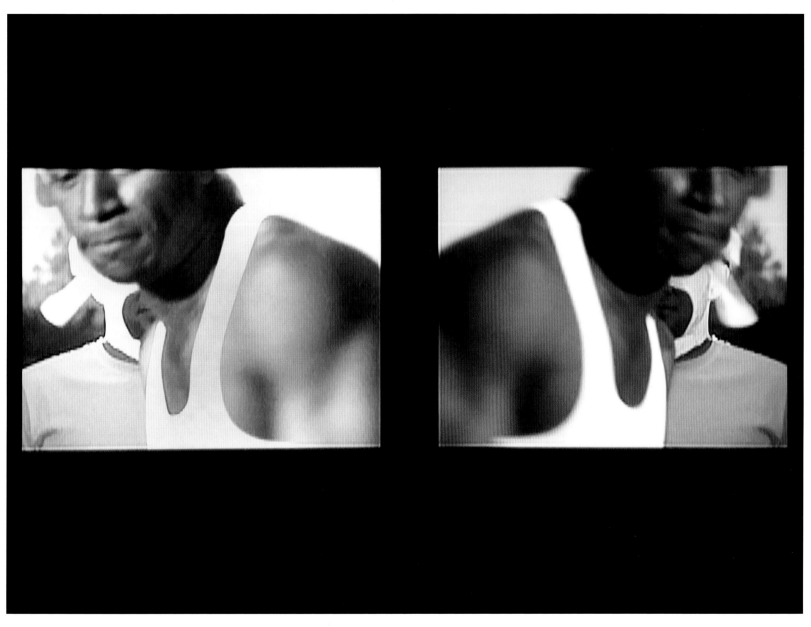

Lauren Woods | *(S)Port of San Francisco* | 2006
3-channel video projection, sound, 6:00 minute loop, each channel

Adrian Piper
Cornered, 1988
Video installation with birth certificates, monitor, table, and chairs
Collection the Museum of Contemporary Art, Chicago, Bernice and Kenneth Newberger Fund, 1190.4.a–p

Tracey Rose
The Wailers, 2004
Digital video projection, color, 6:19 minute loop
Courtesy the artist and the Project, New York

Eve Sandler
The Wash: A Cleaning Story, 1999
Super 8 film, color, sound, 9:00 minutes
Courtesy the artist and Women Make Movies, New York

Berni Searle
Snow White, 2001
Dual video projection with sound, DVD format, shot on DVCAM, 9:24 minute loop

A Matter of Time, 2003
Digital video projection, color, sound, 3:30 minute loop
Both courtesy the artist and Michael Stevenson Gallery, Cape Town

Xaviera Simmons
Landscape: Beach (density), 2005
Digital video, color, 11:14 minute loop
Courtesy the artist

Lorna Simpson
Easy to Remember, 2001
Video projection, 16mm film, black and white, sound, transferred to DVD, 2:35 minute loop
Collection Denver Art Museum, Funds from Norton Foundation, Cathey and Richard Finlon, and Department Acquisition Funds, DAM #2002.89

Cauleen Smith
The Changing Same, 1998–2001
Digital video, color, sound, 5:30 minutes
Courtesy the artist

Pamela Phatsimo Sunstrum
sometimes I answer, 2005
Digital photo animation, color, on two monitors, 1:36 minute loop
Courtesy the artist

Jocelyn Taylor
Armide 2000, 2000
Video, color, sound, 7:00 minute loop
Courtesy the artist

Kara Walker
8 Possible Beginnings or: The Creation of African-America, a Moving Picture by Kara E. Walker, 2005
Video projection, 16mm film, black and white, sound, transferred to DVD, 15:57 minute loop

Testimony: Narrative of a Negress Burdened by Good Intentions, 2004
Video projection, 16mm film, black and white, sound, transferred to DVD, 8:49 minute loop
Both courtesy the artist and Sikkema Jenkins & Co., New York

Carrie Mae Weems
Italian Dreams, 2006
Video, color, sound, 10:35 minute loop
Courtesy the artist and Jack Shainman Gallery, New York

Yvonne Welbon
Monique, 1991
16mm film, color, sound, transferred to DVD, 3:00 minutes
Courtesy the artist and Third World Newsreel, New York

Paula Wilson
Turf, 2005
Oil, woodblock, watercolor, and silica flat on paper and canvas, with video projection
Courtesy the artist and the Artist Pension Trust, New York
Photo courtesy Spelman College Museum of Fine Art, Atlanta

Lauren Woods
(S)Port of San Francisco, 2006
3-channel video projection, sound, 6:00 minute loop, each channel
Courtesy the artist

ART, HISTORY & CULTURE:
SELECT CHRONOLOGY OF BLACK
WOMEN AND THE MOVING IMAGE
Rhea L. Combs

1888   The two-second film *Roundhay Garden Scene*, by Louis Le Prince, is created in Leeds, England. It is considered the earliest surviving motion picture.

1893   Thomas Edison and W. K. L. Dickinson invent the Kinetograph, the first practical moving-picture camera, and the Kinetoscope, an early projector powered by an electrical motor.

1894   Impresario Oscar Hammerstein produces the first public performance of "Living Pictures," at Koster and Bial's Music Hall, in New York. The event includes the rapid projection of a series of photographic images to music.

Edison and Dickinson produce the short film *The Sneeze,* which synchronized the moving image to sound. American inventor Lee DeForest later improves upon this sound-on-film technique.

1910s   The Great Migration, or exodus of blacks, from the American rural South into the industrial North and frontier West, begins. From 1910 until 1930, the total population of blacks in America shifts to more than 20 percent, or approximately one million people, living in the northern and western United States, compared to the 90 percent living in the South immediately following the Emancipation Proclamation.

1914–1918   World War I erupts in Europe. America joins the Great War in 1917, bringing to European shores a large number of African Americans serving in the military.

1915   D. W. Griffith's controversial silent film *Birth of a Nation* becomes a box-office hit. The film receives a glowing endorsement from President Woodrow Wilson, and, in the first eleven months in New York, is seen by an estimated three million people. With its exaggerated depictions of African Americans and romantic portrayal of the Ku Klux Klan, black leaders denounce it as "the meanest vilification of the Negro race."

1916   The genre of race films emerges onto the American landscape and remains active until the late 1940s. Race films, created outside the Hollywood studio system and produced for an all-black audience, feature all-black casts. Oscar Micheaux, Spencer Finch, and the Johnson Brothers, with their Lincoln Production Company, were widely considered the most celebrated and prolific producers of race films; however, such black women filmmakers as Eloyce Gist, Maria P. Williams, and Tressie Souders were also active producers during this period.

1916–1920   Dada, an anti-art cultural movement, emerges in Europe at the height of the Great War and has a profound impact on the development of art practices in the United States. When black GIs bring the improvised nature of jazz to Europe, it radicalizes the work of many artists. One example is filmmaker Oskar Fischinger, who eventually worked for Paramount Pictures and produced the animated films *Allegretto* (1936) and *Fantasia* (1940). These works altered the landscape of film as a medium for experimental expression in mainstream culture.

1918   Racial tension and conflict increase during the first year of the postwar period. Many blacks returning to the United States from military service become increasingly disillusioned by the lukewarm reception and by the country's racial segregation. The Ku Klux Klan expands into northern and midwestern states, and the number of lynchings and other heinous crimes perpetrated against blacks increases, provoking a series of riots in several American cities. The horror of lynching incidents escalates in the ensuing, dark years of America's history.

1920   In the aftermath of the horrific season of race riots, also known as "Red Summer," a group of black intellectuals and literary and visual artists unite in an effort to create a repository of positive and uplifting imagery of blacks. Meta Warrick Fuller creates *Ethiopia Awakening*, which many art historians credit as the first visual manifestation of the birth of the Harlem Renaissance. Other black cultural activities ensue throughout the United States.

An amendment to the United States Constitution provides women with the right to vote. This amendment does not extend to African Americans, however.

1926 Warner Brothers presents the first Vitaphone sound film, *Don Juan.* The sound film is created by photographically recording sound-wave forms onto the filmstrip.

1929 The collapse of the New York Stock Exchange gives rise to the Great Depression in the United States. In the coming decade, more than 25 to 35 percent of the American workforce loses jobs, leaving approximately twelve to fifteen million men, women, and children economically destitute.

1930s *The New York Times* agrees to alter its style manual to capitalize the *N* in Negro.

Zora Neale Hurston, a former student of noted anthropologist Franz Boas, and later an employee of the Works Progress Administration (WPA), conducts many hours of field research in the American South, filming a series of ethnographic films in the process. Her fieldwork scenes are considered the oldest surviving film footage created by an African American woman. Hurston is not alone in her work as a female filmmaker, however. Eslanda Goode Robeson (wife of Paul Robeson), Alice B. Russell (who worked at the Micheaux Film Corporation), and Madam Toussaint Welcome (Booker T. Washington's photographer) also produced a number of artistic, ethnographic, and documentary films over the decade.

1939 The United States enters into World War II. Once again, blacks serve in the military in segregated conditions.

Actress Hattie McDaniel becomes the first African American to win an Academy Award, for her supporting role of "Mammy" in the film *Gone with the Wind.*

1948 Race films all but vanish after the landmark Hollywood antitrust case, which forces the separation of motion picture exhibitors and motion picture production companies. Black actors soon find jobs within the Hollywood system, which later produces such films as *Pinky, Home of the Brave,* and *Carmen Jones.*

1950 *Beulah,* starring Louise Beavers, is the first TV sitcom to star a black actress. It runs for three years. But nothing else of this nature appears on the horizon until 1968, with *Julia.*

1951 Video becomes widely used in the public television broadcast system. Two decades later, in 1972, it is available to the private business sector.

1954 Landmark case of Brown vs Board of Education of Topeka voted unanimously that separate public schools for black and white children was inherently unequal and denied equal rights to blacks. This ruling helped to spawn integration and the Civil Rights movement.

1955 For her performance of the title role in *Carmen Jones,* Dorothy Dandridge is the first black woman to be nominated in the Best Actress category for an Academy Award. She does not win, but the nomination is a milestone and her performance is lauded.

1961 A constellation of artists, later known as NeoDada or Fluxus, emerges in Germany. Drawing upon the earlier principles of Dada, Fluxus extends its reach with the integration of disciplines and the incorporation of new technology. As a consequence, numerous short, experimental films are created and later become known as "Flux films."

1963 Andy Warhol begins working in film. In less than a decade, the prolific artist creates hundreds of short and some feature-length works. They include friends and acquaintances as well as hired models and actors.

Wolf Vostell, a member of NeoDada/Fluxus, is one of the early pioneers to incorporate television and the moving image into his environmental artwork. The exhibition *6 TV de-coll/age* is presented at the Smolin Gallery, in New York.

Ellen Stewart establishes La MaMa Theatre, in New York. It becomes the premier venue for experimental theater and performance art.

Before completing his third year in office, President John F. Kennedy is assassinated in Dallas, Texas.

1964 President Lyndon B. Johnson signs the Civil Rights Act and effectively ends segregation.

1965 Eastman Kodak creates Super 8mm film, also known as Super 8, and commercially releases it on the market. Unable to record sound, Super 8 is still quickly adopted by the amateur filmmaker. Such early users as Nam June Paik, Carolee Schneeman, and Yoko Ono are members of Fluxus.

Fifty years after the Women's Suffrage movement, the Voting Rights Act is passed to protect blacks. Several women, including Ella Baker, Septima Clark, and Fannie Lou Hamer, among many others, work with the civil rights leader Dr. Martin Luther King, Jr., in pressing for its passage.

A weeklong uprising ensues in the Watts area of Los Angeles after a young man, Marquette Frye, is pulled over, allegedly for drunk driving, by a police officer. After the six-day melee, thirty-five people are dead—twenty-five of them black—more than one thousand injured, and six hundred businesses damaged or completely destroyed. Total costs exceed $35 million. The area does not recover.

The University of California, Los Angeles (UCLA), expands its admissions to minority and foreign students; as a result, the university experiences an unprecedented surge in the diversity of its student body.

Activist and community leader Malcolm X, who, a year earlier had made the Muslim pilgrimage to Mecca and changed his name to El-Hajj Malik El-Shabazz, is assassinated in Harlem at the Audubon Ballroom, during a talk to outline his newly formed group, the Organization for African Unity (OAU).

1966 Dakar, Senegal, holds the first World Festival of Negro Arts. African American author W. E. B. Du Bois and scholar Cheikh Diop are honored for influencing African thought in the twentieth century.

The Black Panther Party for Self-Defense, more commonly known as the Black Panther Party (BPP), originates in Oakland, California, and calls for armed resistance against social injustice.

The National Organization for Women (NOW) is formed to eradicate sexual discrimination.

1967 The Sony DVK-2400, also known as the Sony Portapak, becomes commercially available on the consumer market. The inexpensive, handheld camera quickly becomes a favorite of such artists as Vito Acconci, Bruce Nauman, Nam June Paik, and Martha Rosler, among others, who use the medium of video to document performance work. Korean-born Fluxus member Nam June Paik uses the Sony Portapak to shoot footage of Pope Paul VI's processional through New York City. Paik is widely recognized as the first video artist.

Canyon Cinema, a filmmakers' collective specializing in the distribution and presentation of avant-garde and experimental film, is established in Canyon, California, by Bruce Conner, Larry Jordan, and Robert Nelson.

The Los Angeles School forms—also identified by some as "The LA Rebellion." Many African American scholars consider this group the filmic avant-

garde of the 1970s. The most noted filmmakers from this period include Abdosh Abdulhafiz, Melvonna Ballenger, Carroll Parrott Blue, Charles Burnett, Ben Caldwell, Larry Clark, Julie Dash, Zeinabu irene Davis, Jamaa Fanaka, Teshome Gabriel, Haile Gerima, Alile Sharon Larkin, O. Funmilayo Makarah, Barbara McCullough, Bernard Nicholas, and Billy Woodberry.

Newsreel, a collective of radical filmmakers throughout the United States, starts in New York; later, it is known as Third World Newsreel. Its mission—to present the experimental films and videos created by people of color, women, and gay and lesbian filmmakers—has remained unchanged.

Emory Douglas joins the Black Panther Party and becomes the minister of culture. His issue-based, social realistic work defines the agenda of the Panthers, and its art, covering the front and back covers of the Black Panther Party newspaper, is identified as the face of the organization.

1968 In *Julia,* Diahann Carroll becomes the first black star since Louise Beavers, in *Beulah,* to appear in the title role of a TV sitcom. The program dramatizes the adventures of a widow and young mother who relocates to California and moves into a white neighborhood.

Writer Larry Neal, considered one of the principal architects of the Black Arts movement, publishes an article in the *Drama Review* defining the criteria for "black art." Many of its tenets are taken from the pervading black cultural nationalist movement.

Dr. Martin Luther King, Jr., is assassinated on the balcony of the Lorraine Motel in Memphis.

Artist Adrian Piper performs *Meat into Meat* at Loft Performance, in New York. It becomes her first recorded performance work.

Shirley Chisholm becomes the first black woman elected to the United States Congress. She runs for president four years later.

1969 Political activists Bunchy Carter and John Huggins are shot and killed at UCLA, marking the climax of conflict between cultural nationalist organizations within the United Students (US) organization and the Black Panther Party. During this time, scholar Molefi Kete Asante creates his school of thought, Afrocentrism.

FESPACO (Pan-African Film and Television Festival) takes place in Burkina Faso, West Africa. This biannual international exhibition of film and video by artists throughout Africa, North America, Europe, and the

Caribbean becomes the largest and longest running gathering of Pan-African filmmakers.

1970   Gene Youngblood produces the pioneering text *Expanded Cinema,* which discusses pre-1970 computer-generated film. Youngblood has been credited, along with curator Russell Connor, for first using the term *video art* in print.

Connor curates *Vision and Television,* a pioneer museum video-art exhibition, at the Rose Art Museum, Brandeis University, and uses the term "video art" in the catalogue.

Willoughby Sharp curates *Body Works,* an exhibition of single-channel and projected video works by such artists as Vito Acconci, Terry Fox, Dennis Oppenheim, Richard Serra, Keith Sonner, and William Wegman. The show is presented at the Museum of Conceptual Art, in San Francisco.

Madeline Anderson creates the first contemporary film by a black woman, *I Am Somebody.* It examines black women and their supporters at the first mass demonstration after the death of Martin Luther King, Jr.

Women, Students, and Artists for Black Art Liberation (WSABAL) is formed by Faith Ringgold and her daughter, Michele Wallace.

Brothers Dale and Alonzo Davis launch Brockman Gallery Productions, in Los Angeles. It becomes a venue for avant-garde work by African American artists, namely those working in performance like David Hammons, Maren Hassinger, and Senga Nengudi.

1971   Electronic Arts Intermix (EAI) becomes a resource for video art and interactive media. EAI's core program is the international distribution of a major collection of new and historical media works by artists.

Michael Shamberg and the Raindance Foundation produce *Guerrilla Television,* the book that addresses the counterculture phenomenon associated with video art. It features many people involved in early video art and aids in canonizing the art form.

The blaxploitation film is born. Melvin Van Peebles's *Sweet Sweetback's Baadasssss Song* is the exemplar, driven by its hypermasculinity, devastating urban blight, and intense violence.

The Kitchen is established in New York, by Woody and Steina Vasulka. It becomes a venue for video artists and experimental avant-garde performers to exchange ideas.

The work of black women artists is featured in the group exhibition *Where We At: Black Women Artists 1971,* at the Acts of Art Gallery, in New York. From this exhibition, a collective is founded, entitled, simply, Where We At (WWA). The group provides exhibition opportunities for black women who feel marginalized by both the Black Arts movement and the primarily white Feminist movement. In 1972, the group exhibits at the National Conference of Women in the Visual Arts, at different venues in Manhattan. Founding members include Kay Brown, Dindga McCannon, and Faith Ringgold.

1972   The nonprofit organization Women Make Movies begins to promote, distribute, and exhibit independent films and videos by and about women.

1973   The first festival dedicated to women artists, Women's Video Festival, takes place at the University of Illinois, Circle campus, in Chicago.

1974   Linda Goode Bryant founds Just Above Midtown Gallery, in New York. The venue is dedicated to the presentation of experimental and avant-garde work created by African American artists. By the late 1970s, the gallery has presented a series of exhibitions featuring radical new work by such young artists as David Hammons and Senga Nengudi, among others. The exhibition series was encapsulated in the publication *Contextures,* with writings by Linda Goode Bryant and Marcy Phillips.

Women in Film and Video exhibition occurs at the State University of New York, at Buffalo, and includes the work of artists Shirley Clarke, Hermine Freed, Julie Geiger, Jenny Goldberg, Joan Jonas, Sami Klein, Beryl Korot, Shigeko Kubota, Susan Milano, Steina Vasulka, and Jane Wright.

1975   Filmmaker, sculptor, and visual artist Camille Billops, along with her husband, James V. Hatch, establishes the Hatch-Billops Collection, in New York. This extensive collection of African American cultural history includes legions of oral histories, slides, photographs, and other materials documenting African American writers, performers, and visual artists.

1976   Ira Schneider and Beryl Korot coedit *Video Art: An Anthology.* The book gives video artists two pages each to present information about their work, in any manner they choose, and provides useful insight into the ways artists perceive their own work and decide to present it.

1977   As part of his master's thesis assignment from the UCLA film school, Charles Burnett creates *Killer of Sheep,* which examines the Watts section of Los Angeles in the mid-1970s through the eyes of a working-class black family. The National Library of Congress deems this film a National Treasure, and the National Society of Film Critics selects it as one of the "100 Essential Films" of all time.

The Astoria Motion Picture and Television Center Foundation opens in New York. In 1985, the foundation becomes the Museum of the Moving Image.

Frameline begins in San Francisco with a mission to strengthen the visibility of the diverse lesbian, gay, bisexual, and transgender community through artistic expression in film, video, and other media art. Frameline is also home to the San Francisco International LGBT Film Festival, the longest-running, largest, and most widely recognized LGBT film exhibition event in the world.

Senga Nengudi's performance work *Ceremony for Freeway Fets* is presented beneath a Los Angeles Freeway overpass. The performance, a collaboration of Nengudi, Franklin Parker, and Maren Hassinger, is filmed by Barbara McCollough.

1978   LACE (Los Angeles Contemporary Exhibitions) opens and serves as an experimental lab for performance work for artists in Southern California.

1980   Artist and activist Howardena Pindell produces the twelve-minute video *Free, White and 21,* in which she sits in front of a camera and interrogates institutionalized racism and the notion of white privilege.

Independent scholar and film programmer Pearl Bowser presents the work of black women in the retrospective *Black American Independent Cinema 1920–1980* at a festival in Paris.

1981   Camille Billops and James V. Hatch publish the first issue of *Artist and Influence,* an annual publication of writings, poems, and interviews with contemporary musicians, dancers, filmmakers, and visual artists.

The Black Film Center/Archive is established at Indiana University, in Bloomington, as a repository for films and related materials by and about African Americans.

1982   The Black Audio Film Collective is formed in Hackney, London, by John Akomfrah, Reece Auguiste, Edward George, Lina Gopaul, Avril Johnson, David Lawson, and Trevor Mathison. It is one among many such collectives founded in Britain from the early to the mid-1980s, including Ceddo,

ReTake, and the Sankofa Film Collective (founded, in 1984, by artist and filmmaker Isaac Julien).

1986   Digital video becomes available to consumers and is embraced by artists working in experimental video and film.

1988   *Art as a Verb: The Evolving Continuum: Installations, Performances, and Videos by 13 Afro-American Artists* opens at the Maryland Institute College of Art; it later travels to MetLife Gallery and the Studio Museum in Harlem. The exhibition includes work by such artists as Charles Abramson, David Hammons, Maren Hassinger, Candace Hill-Montgomery, Martha Jackson-Jarvis, Senga Nengudi, Lorraine O'Grady, Howardena Pindell, Adrian Piper, Faith Ringgold, Betye Saar, Joyce Scott, and Kaylynn Sullivan.

1990   Digital video becomes a widely accessible medium as QuickTime, Apple computer's architecture for streaming-data format.

1991   Doug Hall and Sally Jo Fifer edit *Illuminating Video: An Essential Guide to Video Art.* The book represents a shift in the discourse on video art. As opposed to explaining what the medium is, it accepts it as an art genre and engages video art within the context of such larger culture questions as race, gender, and sexuality.

1992   Camille Billops and James V. Hatch's film *Finding Christa* receives the Grand Jury Prize for Best Documentary at the Sundance Film Festival.

Julie Dash becomes the first African American woman to have her film, *Daughters of the Dust,* theatrically distributed.

The critical text *Black Popular Culture,* an anthology of writings that is part of the "Discussions in Contemporary Culture" series, is published. Thirty essays, by as many artists, examine issues in film, art, music, television, and other forms of cultural expression.

1994   In London, the Institute for International Visual Arts (inIVA) is established to address an imbalance in the representation of culturally diverse artists, curators, and writers. Over the course of ten years, the organization is successful in launching the careers of many important artists of diverse cultural backgrounds living and working in the United Kingdom and countries throughout Europe.

1996   *New Histories,* an exhibition that explores race and representation, is presented at the Institute of Contemporary Art, Boston. In addition to printed work, the show includes videos by Isaac Julien, Lorraine O'Grady, Kara Walker, and Fred Wilson, among others.

1997 Kara Walker receives the John D. and Catherine T. MacArthur Foundation Achievement Award for her work in visual art.

The 2nd Johannesburg Biennale, under the artistic direction of Okwui Enwesor, comprises a series of exhibitions by noted curators. Kellie Jones features work by women artists. Such film and video artists as Jocelyn Taylor and Carrie Mae Weems are included.

1998 Jacqueline Bobo's groundbreaking anthology, *Black Women Film & Video Artists,* is published.

2000 *Adrian Piper: A Retrospective, 1965–2000* is organized at the New Museum, in New York. The exhibition includes numerous early performance and video works by the artist.

2001 The List Visual Arts Center at MIT presents the exhibition *Race in Digital Space,* organized by Erika Dalya Muhammad. It features the work of more than thirty black artists using film, video, new media, and web techniques. With an emphasis on cultural hybridity, the artists explore how electronic culture influences the production of identity, race, and nationhood.

The Studio Museum in Harlem, in New York, presents the exhibition *Freestyle,* which ushers a new generation of black contemporary artists onto the international art scene.

2002 Lorna Simpson's short film *Easy to Remember* debuts at the Whitney Biennial.

Camille Billops and James V. Hatch gift Emory University part of the Hatch-Billops Collection. The archive becomes the Camille Billops and James V. Hatch Archive at Emory University.

The exhibition *One Planet Under a Groove: Hip Hop and Contemporary Art* is organized at the Bronx Museum, in New York. It features work by contemporary black artists who draw on the thematic and artistic lexicon of hip hop culture, including the iconic rap video.

2003 Filmmaker Yvonne Welbon releases her documentary *Sisters in Cinema,* and starts a website of the same name (www.sistersincinema.com), to illustrate the long-standing history of black women in film and video.

Conceptual and performance artist Damali Ayo launches her satirical website, rent-a-negro.com, which uses interactions between blacks and whites to examine racism. In the first month, the site receives more than four hundred thousand hits per day.

2004 Halle Berry is the first black woman in the category of Best Actress to win an Academy Award, for *Monster's Ball.*

2005 *Creating Their Own Image: The History of African American Women Artists,* by art historian Lisa E. Farrington, is published. The book includes interviews and works by black American women artists, from slavery to the present.

Double Consciousness: Black Conceptual Art Since 1970 is presented at the Contemporary Arts Museum Houston, and features early work by Maren Hassinger, Senga Nengudi, Howardena Pindell, and Adrian Piper.

The Studio Museum in Harlem, following up on the critical acclaim for *Freestyle,* presents an equally dynamic exhibition of young black artists titled *Frequency.* It features the work of Zoë Charlton, Xaviera Simmons, and Paula Wilson.

2006 *Lorna Simpson,* a twenty-year survey of the artist's work, is organized by the American Federation of Arts and travels throughout the United States.

Jennifer Hudson wins Best Supporting Actress for *Dreamgirls* at the 79th Academy Awards.

2007 *WACK! Art and the Feminist Revolution,* organized by the Museum of Contemporary Art, Los Angeles, and *Global Feminism,* organized by the Brooklyn Museum, are unveiled. Each chronicles the origins and presentation of feminist artmaking from a national and international perspective, respectively. The exhibitions feature the collective WWA and such black women artists as Senga Nengudi, Lorraine O'Grady, Howardena Pindell, and Adrian Piper.

ARTISTS' BIOGRAPHIES
Compiled by Makeba G. Dixon-Hill and Anne Collins Smith

INA DIANE ARCHER
(b. 1962, American; lives and works in New York)
Ina Diane Archer, a video artist, received a BFA in film and video from the Rhode Island School of Design, an MA in cinema studies from New York University, and participated in the Independent Study Program at the Whitney Museum of American Art, New York. She was artist in residence at Film/Video Arts, New York, and has received awards from Harvestworks Digital Media Arts Center, New York (2001) and the Creative Capital Foundation, New York (2005).

Particularly interested in innovative early sound cinema and musical comedies, Archer is an advocate for the preservation of film, often using vintage examples to challenge racial ethnicity in the classics. For instance, in *1/16th of 100%?!* (1993–96) she examines themes of appropriation, miscegenation, and minstrelsy by manipulating movie footage from the 1920s through the 1950s, including such features as *Imitation of Life, Show Boat,* and *The Jazz Singer.* Archer also inserts herself into some of her film-based work to raise questions about who is excluded and included in the pantheon of American cinema. *Hattie McDaniel: or A Credit to the Motion Picture Industry* (2002) investigates an error in a media clip from the 1939 Academy Awards, at which Hattie McDaniel won Best Supporting Actress for *Gone with the Wind,* and suggests that her speech was restaged and the footage reshot.

Archer's videos have been presented in the Whitney Independent Study Open Studios Show (1997); the traveling exhibition *Race in Digital Space* (2001–3); *Eve,* Rush Arts Gallery, New York (2004); *Veni Vidi Video,* Studio Museum in Harlem, New York (2004); *How It Feels/Where It's At,* video installation, Heidi Cho Gallery, New York (2005); *Currents: African American Video Art Today,* Cheekwood Museum of Art, Nashville (2005); *Florent's Bi-Decadent Retrospective,* White Columns, New York (2005); and *Dangling Between the Real Thing and the Sign in the Window,* Dam, Stuhltrager Gallery, Brooklyn (2006).

Archer's films have been screened at such festivals as the NYU-SCE Filmmakers Networks Festival II, Anthology Film Archive, New York (1992); Women of Color Film Festival, Santa Cruz, California (1996); First Annual New York Women's Film Festival (1997); and the List Visual Arts Center, MIT, Cambridge, Massachusetts (2001).   [ACS]

ELIZABETH AXTMAN
(b. 1980, American; lives and works in Oakland, California)
Elizabeth Axtman is a photographer and video artist. She received her BFA from San Francisco State University in 2004 and completed her MFA in photography, film, video, and new media at the School of the Art Institute of Chicago in 2006. She was also a participant in the Skowhegan School of Painting and Drawing 2006 Summer Residency Program.

Axtman joins a group of young cultural producers and critical thinkers who engage the African American experience through myriad historical and popular references that seek to turn the dialogue on race and gender on its head. Her video and photo-based works engage race and power in the contemporary age. Steeped in humor, defiance, and confrontation, Axtman's explorations provide meditations on the "tragic mulatto" character (*American Classics,* 2005), give her opportunities to infiltrate traditionally restricted spaces (*Where's The Party At?,* 2006), and allow her to insert personal commentary in historical events (*Expletives Owed,* 2007).

She has participated in exhibitions and festivals at the Renaissance Society of the University of Chicago, Gene Siskel Film Center Gallery,

Gallery 2, and Woman Made Gallery, in Chicago; Diaspora Vibe Gallery, Miami; Arthouse, Austin, Tex.; 10th Annual Maine International Film Festival, Waterville; and San Francisco State University and Legion of Honor, San Francisco. She has lectured at the School of the Art Institute of Chicago and the San Francisco Art Institute, and is a recipient of the Skowhegan Endowment for Scholarship Foundation.   [MDH]

CAMILLE BILLOPS
(b. 1933, American; lives and works in New York)
Camille Billops is a multifaceted artist, ceramist, filmmaker, printmaker, and custodian of African American culture. She received a BA from Los Angeles State College (1960), an MFA from City College, City University of New York (1973), and studied printmaking with the renowned artist-printmaker Robert Blackburn at the Blackburn Printmaking Studio, New York.

Billops's family-based autobiographical docudramas—*Suzanne, Suzanne* (1982), *Older Women and Love* (1987), *Finding Christa* (1991), *Take Your Bags* (1998), and *A String of Pearls* (2002)—examine complex family relationships, concentrating on the effects of child and drug abuse, countercultural romantic relationships, adoption, slavery, the Middle Passage, and the struggles of the men in her family. Her film *The KKK Boutique Ain't Just Rednecks* (1994), loosely based on Dante's *Inferno,* satirically confronts the complexities of covert racism.

Billops's films have received the Sundance Film Festival Grand Jury Prize for Documentaries (1992) and Best Documentary awards from the Black Maria Film Festival (1994) and the National Black Programming Consortium. She has also received an Obie Award for her Off-Broadway theater work (1997). She is the recipient of the James Van Der Zee Award from the Brandywine Graphics Workshop, Philadelphia (1994), Governor's Award from the Skowhegan School of Painting and Sculpture (2000), and National Women's Caucus for Art Lifetime Achievement Award (2002).

Beyond her artistic achievements, Billops is also a consummate archivist and publisher. In 1975, she established the Hatch-Billops Collection with her husband, literary critic and writer James V. Hatch. The collection is an important archive of African American cultural history—artwork, books, interviews, oral histories, poetry, reference materials, slides, and special collections. The collection also publishes the annual journal *Artist and Influence,* which contains interviews with performing and visual artists. The journal provides important information about the role of minorities in the development of American arts. Billops and Hatch have donated portions of their collection to the Black Film Center/Archive at Indiana University and to the Camille Billops and James V. Hatch Archives at Emory University.   [ACS]

CARROLL PARROTT BLUE
(b. 1943, American; lives and works in Houston)
Carroll Parrott Blue is a world-renowned author, educator, and filmmaker whose work during the 1980s and '90s positioned her as an integral figure in African American documentary film production. Blue received her BA in English literature from Boston University and MFA in motion picture production from the University of California, Los Angeles. She also was the recipient of numerous fellowships, sponsored by the American Film Institute, Coro Foundation, and Corporation for Public Broadcasting, among many others, and is currently a visiting scholar in the African American studies department of the University of Houston.

Blue's early documentaries focus on women of the African Diaspora. Following upon her ten-minute documentary film *Two Women* (1976), *Varnette's World: A Study of a Young Artist* (1979) profiles the life and work of visual artist Varnette Honeywood. Concentrating once again on the visual arts, Blue also wrote, produced, and directed *Conversations with Roy DeCarava* (1982) and *Nigerian Art—Kindred Spirits* (1990). *Eyes on the Prize, Series II* (1989) and *Black Is . . . Black Ain't* (1992), works she segment- and field-produced, respectively, emerged as seminal visual texts that link numerous voices and stories particular to the African American experience.

Her 2003 memoir, *Dawn at My Back: Memoir of a Texas Upbringing, An Interactive Cultural History,* conflates music, technology, prose, and visual imagery in a rich narrative that documents her relationship with her mother, in Houston, during segregation. Employing the voices of local Houston historians, multidisciplinary artist Debbie Allen, and actors Ruby Dee and Ossie Davis, Blue's narrative, which is not only a book but a website and a DVD, elevates the author's journey and gives it a personal, collective, and artistic identity. Embarking upon collaborations with Albert Chu, Leamon Green, and Sharon Johnston, *The Dawn Project,* in the form of public art and media installations, will be on view at five public transit stations in Houston until 2012.

Blue's creative experience has spanned more than thirty years. She has also held teaching posts at San Diego State University, the University of Central Florida, Indiana University, California State Polytechnic University, and several departments within the University of Houston. Her still photography has been included in major exhibitions at the Art Institute of Pittsburgh; Corcoran Gallery of Art, Washington, D.C.; San Francisco Museum of Modern Art; Studio Museum in Harlem, New York; and University of Texas, Austin.   [MDH]

MARÍA MAGDALENA CAMPOS-PONS
(b. 1959, Cuban; lives and works in Boston)
María Magdalena Campos-Pons is a Cuban expatriate multimedia artist of Yoruban ancestry living in North America. She combines elements of installation, painting, photography, performance, and video to relate her experiences as an expatriate. Her rich cultural heritage informs and influences her aesthetic and artistic investigation of dislocation, femininity, identity, longing, and spirituality.

Originally educated in traditional painting, Campos-Pons began to incorporate installation, performance, and video while a student at Massachusetts College of Art. This new media was a natural progression in her work; it allowed her to integrate Santeria spiritual traditions and ritual.

The artist has been the subject of solo exhibitions, including *History of People Who Were Not Heroes,* Bunting Institute of Radcliffe College, Harvard University (1994); *When I Am Not Here. Estoy Alla,* Caribbean Cultural Center, New York (1997); *Spoken Softly with Mama,* Museum of Modern Art, New York, and National Gallery of Canada, Ottawa (1998); *Meanwhile the Girls Were Playing,* List Visual Arts Center, MIT, Cambridge, Massachusetts (1999–2000); a self-titled exhibition, Gallery Pack, Milan (2002); *One Thousand Ways to Say Goodbye,* Henie Onstad, Kunstsenter, Oslo (2003); *3X3 Threads of Memory,* Dak'Art, Dakar Biennale, Senegal (2004); *Backyard Dreams,* Julie Saul Gallery, New York (2005); and the midcareer retrospective *María Magdalena Campos-Pons: Everything Is Separated by Water,* Indianapolis Museum of Art (2007).

Among Campos-Pons's group exhibitions are *Africa in America,* a traveling exhibition from the 4th Biennale of Havana, National Museum of Fine Arts (1991); *Trade Routes,* Johannesburg Biennale (1997); *Authentic/Ex-centric: Africa in and Out Africa,* 49th Venice Biennale (2001); *Unpacking Europe,* Museum Boijmans Van Beuningen, Rotterdam (2001); *Ritual Acts Videos by Women,* DeCordova Museum, Lincoln, Massachusetts (2002); *Only Skin Deep,* International Center of Photography, New York (2003); *Dreaming Now,* Rose Art Museum, Brandeis University (2005); *Pan African Exhibition of Contemporary Art,* Museum of

Modern Art, Salvador Bahia, Brazil (2005); *Getting Emotional,* Institute of Contemporary Art, Boston (2005); *Backyard Dreams,* Julie Saul Gallery, New York (2005); *Transplant-Transculture,* Glyndor Gallery, Wave Hill Public Garden and Cultural Center, Bronx (2006); and *Dispersed,* Museum of the African Diaspora, San Francisco (2006).

Campos-Pons studied painting at the National School of Art and Higher Institute of Art, Havana, and media arts at Massachusetts College of Art. She has served as visiting artist and artist in residence at Polaroid, in Boston (1997, 2000); Photographers Gallery, Saskatoon, Canada (1997); Rutgers University Center for Innovative Print and Paper, New Brunswick, New Jersey (1997); and Bunting Institute of Radcliffe College, Harvard University (1997).   [ACS]

ZOË CHARLTON

(b. 1973, American; lives and works in Washington, D.C.)
Zoë Charlton is an artist who works in the media of drawing, installation, and video. She earned a BA in studio art from Florida State University, Tallahassee, and an MFA in painting from the University of Texas, Austin.

Charlton's drawings portray scantily clad or nude African American women. Their identity, often obscured by such items as a white Ku Klux Klan hood, white face paint, or a party hat, is an attempt to examine the politics of gender, class, and the historical events that continue to inform society today. She explores race and sex in America and the commoditization of identity; her video-based work addresses issues of self-preservation, the male gaze, and the subjectivity of the black female body. Charlton explains that her "investigation of stereotypical imagery challenges my audience to question and transcend racist character concepts and to realize that negative racial stereotypes do not help to define individuals."

Zoë Charlton's work has been featured in solo and two-person exhibitions, including *Menagerie of Mediocrity* (collaboration with Nathan Pasco), Oglesby Gallery, Tallahassee, Florida (1995); *Change in My Pocket,* featuring a performance of *The Pressifixtion,* New Gallery, Austin, Texas (1998); *There Goes the Neighborhood* (collaboration with Rick Delaney), Cox Gallery, Springfield, Missouri (2004); *The Quest: New Work by Zoë Charlton,* Watkins Gallery, American University, Washington, D.C. (2004); Creative Alliance, Baltimore (2004); Wendy Cooper Gallery, Chicago (2006); Clementine Gallery, New York (2006); and *Saint in the Suburb,* University of North Texas Art Gallery, Denton (2007).

Among Charlton's group exhibitions are *Mostra D'Arte,* Centro Studi Santa Chiara, Castiglion Fiorentino, Italy (1998); in Texas, *The Question of Race,* Bridge Center for Contemporary Art, El Paso (2000), *Out of the Ordinary,* Contemporary Arts Museum Houston (2000), *Women & Their Work,* Austin (2000, 2001), and *Beyond the Academy: Encouraging New Talent from Texas,* Galveston Arts Center (2003); *(In)visible Silence,* Drawing Center, New York (2004); *Veni, Vidi, Video* (2004) and *Frequency* (2005), Studio Museum in Harlem, New York; *Made in Na Ma,* Contemporary Artists Center, North Adams, Mass. (2005); *Black Alphabet,* Zacheta National Gallery of Art, Warsaw (2006); and *This Ain't No Karaoke,* Haas & Fischer Gallery, Zurich (2006).

She has participated in artist residencies at the Haystack Mountain School of Crafts, Deer Isle, Maine (1990); Skowhegan School of Painting and Sculpture (2001); Creative Alliance, Baltimore (2003); Contemporary Artists Center, North Adams, Massachusetts (2005); and Springfield Pottery, Springfield, Missouri (2006).   [ACS]

AYOKA CHENZIRA

(American; lives and works in Atlanta)

Ayoka Chenzira is an award-winning filmmaker and digital media artist whose productions embrace drama, animation, documentaries, performance art, and experimental narrative productions. Trained in dance, painting, still photography, music, film, and video, she received a BFA in film production from New York University and an MA in education from Columbia University's Teachers College.

Over her thirty-year career, Chenzira has written, directed, and produced fifteen films and short-subject digital projects, including *Syvilla: They Dance to Her Drum* (1979), *Hair Piece: A Film for Nappyheaded People* (1984), *Secret Sounds Screaming: The Sexual Abuse of Children* (1986), and *In the Rivers of Mercy Angst* (1996). Her commercially released film *Alma's Rainbow* (1994) is one of the first 35mm films written, produced, and directed by an African American woman to appear on *Billboard's* top-forty home-video sales list.

Chenzira is the recipient of numerous awards, including the Sony Innovator Award for her early work with converging film, video, and computer animation; the Cultural Affairs Award from the National Black Programming Consortium; designation by New Jersey's Newark Museum as one of the most important African American filmmakers of the twentieth century (2000); Atlanta's Black Women's Film Preservation Society Trailblazer Award (2002); and the Distinguished Educator Award from Apple Computer for her work with storytelling and digital technology (2003).

As an educator, Chenzira distinguished herself at the City College of New York, where she served as chair of the department of media and communication arts and cocreated the MFA program in Media Arts Production, the first graduate-level program of its kind at a public institution in New York. She was the first William and Camille Cosby Endowed Chair of Fine Arts at Spelman College, and is the creator and director of its Digital Moving Image Salon (DMIS). She is completing a PhD program in digital media at Georgia Institute of Technology.

Ayoka Chenzira is currently working on a digital media project in which she is developing "tangible narratives." The project uses sensing technologies embedded into sculpture and incorporates photography, film, and video to create and reframe various types of narratives. She recently wrote and directed the film *HER,* one of the first science-fiction works to be written, produced, and directed by a team of African American women.   [ACS]

OGECHI CHIEKE

(b. 1981, American; lives and works in New York)

Ogechi Chieke is a multimedia artist whose productions encompass performance art, dance, film, and animation. She received her BFA in electronic studio art from Howard University and her MFA in computer arts at the School of Visual Arts, New York.

In her work, Chieke projects her personal intuitive perspectives onto physical and historical ideas concerning identity and the human condition. Often incorporating references to science fiction, music, and the black radical imagination, she uses body painting and innovative filmmaking techniques to accentuate the beauty and oddity of the human form. Exploring themes of mythology and creation stories, artistic process and popular recognition, Chieke employs various methods of reformatting technology to mimic two-dimensional textures, create visual and aural illusions, and depict aged cinematic formats.

Her work has been exhibited at Rush Arts Gallery, New York University, and the Mushroom Arts Gallery, in New York; Studio 15 Gallery, and Howard University Art Gallery, in Washington, D.C.; Three Rivers Arts

Festival and Yoga Sadhana Gallery, in Pittsburgh; and the Soap Factory, in Minneapolis. [MDH]

JULIE DASH
(b. 1952, American; lives and works in Los Angeles)
Julie Dash is a multifaceted artist whose extensive work as director, writer, editor, producer, and educator has cemented her position as an integral figure in American cinema, cultural studies, and entrepreneurship. Dash's academic education includes fellowships at the American Film Institute's Center for Advanced Film Studies and its conservatory at Greystone Mansion, Los Angeles, a BA in film production from the City College of New York, and an MFA in film and television production from the University of California, Los Angeles. She cites a film production workshop conducted at the Studio Museum in Harlem as one of her early, and memorable, academic experiences in film.

Dash is credited as an innovator for her subject matter, identification of artistic talent, use of film stock, and pioneering strategies in gaining film distribution, demonstrated in her strong interest in the metanarratives that exist among black female communities in the United States. Two films, in particular, emerge: the critically acclaimed short *Illusions* (1983) and the feature-length *Daughters of the Dust* (1992). *Illusions* provides a commentary that counters popular culture's perception of black women and their contributions to American cinema. Set in the 1940s, one year after the attack on Pearl Harbor, the film documents the friendship of two women and their individual struggles, all taking place in a Hollywood motion picture studio. Nine years later, her most popular commercial release, *Daughters of the Dust,* chronicles the collective life of the Peazant family through the voices, primarily, of the female family members. This work positioned Dash as the first African American woman to have a full-length general theatrical release in the United States.

Dash's films have received numerous awards and accolades: Best Film of the Decade, by the Black Filmmakers Foundation, for *Illusions;* an NAACP Image Award for *The Rosa Parks Story;* and, for *Daughters of the Dust,* inclusion into the National Film Registry, *Filmmakers' Magazine* list of one of the fifty most important independent films ever made, Sundance Film Festival award for Best Cinematography, and being cited as one of the most important cinematic achievements of the twentieth century at the 25th Annual Black Film Festival. Dash also directs music videos, commercials, television series' episodes, and movies.

Her involvement with cultural institutions was also realized in her short film *Brothers of the Borderland* (2004), created specifically for one of five inaugural exhibitions at the National Underground Railroad Freedom Center Museum, in Cincinnati. In addition to guest-lecturing at numerous prestigious colleges and universities throughout the United States, Dash manages her own website, Geechee Girls Multimedia. [MDH]

ZEINABU *irene* DAVIS
(b. 1961, American; lives and works in San Diego)
Zeinabu irene Davis is an independent filmmaker who employs narrative, documentary, silent cinema, and experimental tenets in her film and video work. Her films have tackled such issues as racial and gender inequality, intergenerational friendships, motherhood, and the intimate relationships that occur between black men and women.

Davis's first feature-length motion picture, *Compensation* (1999), emerged as a landmark production that went on to influence new trends in film, both on- and offscreen. Inspired by the Paul Lawrence Dunbar poem, also titled *Compensation* (1906), Davis portrays two love stories, both involving a deaf woman and a hearing man, spanning two different eras in Chicago. Garnering stellar print reviews for its multilayered language techniques, employment of deaf actors and technicians, and on-screen portrayal of black deaf culture, *Compensation* provided further opportunities for Davis's work to be seen by diverse audiences, including African American deaf communities, mainstream audiences, and commercial audiences.

Davis has worked as editor, producer, actor, consultant, and director in the film industry for more than two decades and has received numerous accolades—from the Toronto Film Festival, National Black Programming Consortium, Independent Film Project, Black Film Video Network, and Sundance Film Festival. She is also the recipient of funding grants from the National Endowment for the Arts, Rockefeller Foundation, and American Film Institute.

In addition to screening her films and videos at various festivals, Davis's work has been exhibited at the Museum of Contemporary Art, Chicago, Princeton University, and the Indianapolis Museum of Art. A writer and lecturer on African diasporic cinema, she is a professor of communication at the University of California, San Diego.   [MDH]

STEPHANIE DINKINS

(b. 1964, American; lives and works in Brooklyn)
Stephanie Dinkins is an interdisciplinary artist who combines video with organic and found materials to create hybrid sculptures and installations. She has received a BS in marketing and advertising, Syracuse University, New York, an MFA in photography, Maryland Institute College of Art, a Certificate in Photography, International Center of Photography, New York, and participated in the Independent Study Program at the Whitney Museum of American Art, New York.

Dinkins's mixed-media installations explore issues of value and visibility. They have been featured in such solo exhibitions as *Searching for the Here & Now,* Maryland Institute College of Art (1997); *One World* (1994) and *The End Is the Beginning and Lies Far Ahead* (1999), Snug

Harbor Cultural Center, Staten Island, New York; *Survive/Thrive/Alive,* Glyndor Gallery, Wave Hill, Bronx (2006); and *The End Is the Beginning and Lies Far Ahead, #IV,* Marygrove College, Detroit, (2007). The artist's site-specific installations have been on view at the Art/Omi International Arts Center, Omi, New York (1999); Castle Cimelice, Foundation and Center for Contemporary Arts, Cimelice, Czech Republic (2001); Williamsburg Art and Historical Center, Brooklyn (2001); and Gallery North, Long Island, New York (2001).

Among the group exhibitions in which Dinkins's work has appeared are *Kongo Criollo,* Taller Boricua Gallery, New York (1998); *Combio Constante III,* Monasterio de Veruela, Zaragoza, Spain (2002); *Pilgrimage,* Bronx River Art Center, Bronx, New York (2002); *Socle du Monde Biennial Exhibition,* Herning Kunstmuseum, Copenhagen (2002); *[B L A N K]: In Search of An American History,* SAC Gallery, State University of New York, Stony Brook (2003); *Veni Vidi Video II,* Studio Museum in Harlem, New York (2004); *The Sun Never Sets,* SAC Gallery, State University of New York, Stony Brook, (2005); *Afrofuturism,* Soap Factory, Minneapolis (2005); *Artificial Africa,* GAS (Gigantic Art Space), New York (2006); *Socle du Monde Revisited,* Herning Kunstmuseum, Copenhagen (2006); and *Reparations,* SAC Gallery, State University of New York, Stony Brook (2007).

Dinkins participated in artist residencies at the Art/Omi International Arts Center, Omi, New York (1999); Anderson Center for Interdisciplinary Studies, Red Wing, Minnesota (2000); Foundation and Center for Contemporary Art, Prague (2001); Monesterio de Veruela, Zaragoza, Spain (2001); Snug Harbor Cultural Center, Staten Island, New York (2001); Sanita Comfort Footwear Company, Ikast, Denmark (2002); and Santa Fe Art Institute, New Mexico (2007).   [ACS]

Gaiter's work has been the subject of solo exhibitions, including *easily remembered/conveniently forgotten,* Benedicta Art Center, College of St. Benedict, St. Joseph, Minnesota (1993), and *SPACE/RACE* (1998), at the Institute of Visual Art, University of Milwaukee; CSPS Contemporary Arts Center, Cedar Rapids, Iowa; and Project Row Houses, Houston.

Among her group exhibitions are *What Will You Miss?,* School of Art and Design Gallery, Georgia State University, Atlanta (1999); *Sources,* Macalester College Art Gallery, St. Paul, Minnesota (1999); *Who Knows Where or When: Artists Interpret Geography and Time,* Charles A. Wustum Museum of Fine Arts, Racine, Wisconsin (2000); and *Our New Day Begun: African American Artists Entering the Millennium,* Lyndon Baines Johnson Library, Austin, Texas (2000). Gaiter is associate professor of new media and graphic design at the University of Delaware.   [ACS]

LEAH GILLIAM
(b. 1967, American; lives and works in Annandale-on-Hudson, New York)
Leah Gilliam explores racial and sexual differences through the medium of the moving image. She received her BA from Brown University in 1989 and MFA in film from the University of Wisconsin, Milwaukee, in 1992. Gilliam is currently director of the Integrated Arts Program and associate professor in the Film and Electronic Arts Program at Bard College.

Citing the collection of found objects as a central component of her artistic practice, Gilliam considers the repurposing of old images and obsolete technology integral to a discussion on the future—and human-kind's place in it. While she is most celebrated for her film and video work—*Sapphire and the Slave Girl* (1995), featured in the 1997 Whit-ney Biennial, and *Apeshit* (1999), voted Best of 1999 by *Film Comment* magazine—her medium has evolved to include digital processing, image manipulation, and nonlinear, web-based narration to recontextualize futuristic concepts of history and race from the perspective of problem-atic film footage, such as the parallel between African Americans and primates.

Gilliam's new media work has been presented at the New Museum of Contemporary Art, Studio Museum in Harlem, and Thread Waxing Space Gallery, in New York, and the List Visual Arts Center, MIT, Cam-bridge, Massachusetts. Her *Sapphire and the Slave Girl* won the New Visions Video Award at the San Francisco International Film Festival. Gilliam has participated in public programs at the Lower Manhattan Cul-tural Council and New York Underground Film Festival, and at Cornell University, Pomona College, and DePaul University, among others. She has received grants and fellowships from the National Endowment for the Arts, Creative Capital, Bard College, and the Center for New Televi-sion. In addition, her work is included in collections at Duke University, Smith College, the University of Chicago, Indiana University, and the University of California, at both Irvine and Santa Cruz.   [MDH]

RENÉE GREEN
(b. 1959, American; lives and works in San Francisco)
Renée Green, artist, filmmaker, and writer, received a BA from Wesleyan University, studied at the School of Visual Arts, New York, and completed the Independent Study Program at the Whitney Museum of American Art, New York. Her work investigates circuits of relation and exchange over time, the gaps and shifts in what survives in public and private mem-ories, as well as what has been imagined and invented via architecture, digital media, films, installations, sound-related works, and writing.

In such early installations as *Sa Main Charmant* (1989) and *Revue* (1990), Green shows how women of African descent have been viewed throughout history, and, in particular, the European fascination with, and exoticization of, Saartje Baartman and Josephine Baker. Other works, including *Import/Export Funk Office* (1992) and *WaveLinks* (2000–2004), explore cultural theory, media and communication, and music's capacity to link people and time periods. Utilizing image, sound, and text, she employs an anthropological approach to such issues as existence, meaning, memory, racial classification, and human subjectivity.

Green's work has been presented in solo exhibitions: *Import/Export Funk Office,* Galerie Christian Nagel, Cologne (1992); *Wiener Secession,* Vienna (1999); *Sombras y Senales,* Fundació Antoní Tàpies, Barcelona (2000); *Phrases and Versions,* Portikus, Frankfurt (2002–3); *Elsewhere? Here,* Galeria Filomena Soares, Lisbon (2004); *Renée Green,* Contemporary Arts Center, Cincinnati (2004); *Relay,* Kunstraum Innsbruck (2005); Galleria Emi Fontana, Milan (2005); *Index (From Oblivion): Paradoxes and Climates,* Einstein Spaces, Berlin (2005); *Unité d'habitation,* Galerie Martine Aboucaya, Paris (2006); and *Wavelinks,* Neuberger Museum of Art, State University of New York, Purchase (2006).

Among the group exhibitions in which Green's work has been featured are *Out of Site,* P.S. 1 Contemporary Art Center, Long Island City, New York (1990); 1993 Whitney Biennial, Whitney Museum of American Art, New York (1993); 45th Venice Biennale (1993); *Parasite,* Drawing Center, New York (1998); Documenta XI, Kassel (2002); *Strangers: The First International Center of Photography Triennial,* International Center of Photography, New York (2003); *18/20 la fin du XVIIIe siècle aujourd'hui,* Ancien Musée de Peinture, Grenoble (2004); *Double Consciousness: Black Conceptual Art Since 1970,* Contemporary Arts Museum Houston (2005); 2nd Bienal Internacional de Arte Contemporáneo de Sevilla, Spain (2006); *Simply Red,* Fabric Workshop and Museum, Philadelphia (2007); *Cinema Cavern,* P.S. 1 Contemporary Art Center, Long Island City, New York (2007); and the 10th International Istanbul Biennial (2007). Green is currently dean of graduate programs at the San Francisco Art Institute. [ACS]

MARGUERITE HARRIS
(b. 1964, American; lives and works in San Francisco)
Marguerite Harris is a visual artist, poet, and writer who received a BA in telecommunications and film criticism and theory from Indiana University, Bloomington, and both a BFA in film and an MFA in new media from San Francisco Art Institute. Her installations are inspired by such conceptual artists as Peter Campus, Yoko Ono, and Adrian Piper. Other artists who inform her work are the conceptual filmmakers Dakota Dehinde, Shirley Shor, Scott Snibbe, and Jennifer Steinkamp, who incorporate digital media in their installation-based work.

Harris explains: "Most of my work including video is installation. These new-media environments explore space, structure, body, time, and movement." Influenced by conceptual art practice with references to ethnic identity, Harris appreciates how materials are used. She has combined her affinity for new media and materials with her hand-made film *Flowers & Leaves* (2001), which is accompanied by etchings of photographic stills from the film.

Harris's photographs and videos have been presented at the *Northern National Art Competition,* Nicolet Area Technical College, Rhinelander, Wisconsin (1995); *Photographers,* Campbell Steele Gallery, Marion, Iowa (1996); DeRicci Gallery, Edgewood College, Madison, Wisconsin (1997); ARC Gallery, Chicago (1997); Intermedia Arts, Minneapolis (1997); Walker Art Center, Minneapolis (1998); *Microsoft Show,* One Market Street, San Francisco (2001); Diego Gallery, San Francisco Art Institute (2000, 2002, 2003); 2004 *MFA Thesis Show,* Herbst Pavilion-Fort Mason, San Francisco (2004); and *Collectif Jeune Cinema, Installation Exhibit,* Paris (2006, 2007). [ACS]

MAREN HASSINGER

(b. 1947, American; lives and works in Baltimore)

Maren Hassinger, a multimedia artist who creates sculpture and installation, performance, and video art, received a BA from Bennington College and an MFA from the University of California, Los Angeles. She is well regarded for her public art projects: the installations *Twelve Trees #2,* San Diego Freeway, Los Angeles (1979); *Window Boxes,* Whitney Museum at Philip Morris, New York (1993); *Fence of Leaves,* P.S. 8, New York (1995); *Ancestor Walk,* P.S. 176, New York (1996); *Message from Malcolm,* 110th Street IRT subway station, New York (2001); and *Art in the Garden,* Grant Park, Chicago (2004–5).

Hassinger uses natural and industrial materials to create works that look like branches, bushes, and trees in her sculpture and installations. Her work is concerned with the viewer's experience and relationship to nature. Although she used video to document her performances, a 1991 move to Long Island, New York, prompted her to experiment with video and to incorporate it as an independent medium. Maureen Megerian's 1997 article on Hassinger, "Entwined with Nature," in the *Women's Art Journal,* explains that the artist's video-based work "explores a sense of place and family amidst surrounding nature." Hassinger's later video work has taken on a more highly charged tone, as with the performance-based video *daily mask* (2004).

Among her solo exhibitions are *Gallery Six: Maren Hassinger,* Los Angeles County Museum of Art (1981); Los Angeles City College Art Gallery (1985); *Focus: Environment, Maren Hassinger,* California State University Art Gallery, Northridge (1985); *Blanket of Branches* and *Dancing Branches,* Contemporary Arts Forum and Alice Keck Park, Santa Barbara, California (1986); self-titled exhibition at Gracie Mansion Gallery, New York (1991); *Memory,* Benton Gallery, Southampton, New York (1993); *Treachery and Consolation,* Trans-Hudson Gallery, Jersey City, New Jersey (1996); *My hand, this leaf,* David Allen Gallery, Brooklyn (2001); *Diaries,* Julio Art Gallery, Loyola College, Baltimore (2004); *Rainforest,* David Allen Gallery, Brooklyn (2004); and *The River,* School 33, Baltimore (2005).

Maren Hassinger has participated in numerous group exhibitions, among them *The Decade Show,* New Museum of Contemporary Art, New York (1990); *Passages,* Studio Museum in Harlem, New York (1999); *Double Consciousness: Black Conceptual Art Since 1970,* Contemporary Arts Museum Houston (2005); *City Art: New York's Percent for Art Program,* Center for Architecture, New York (2005); and *Along the Way: MTA Arts for Transit, Celebrating 20 Years of Public Art,* UBS Art Gallery, New York (2005). Her work has been presented in such traveling exhibitions as *Forever Free: Art by African American Women, 1862–1980,* Illinois State University, Normal (1981); *Art as a Verb: The Evolving Continuum,* Maryland Institute College of Art (1988); and *Bearing Witness: Contemporary Works by African American Women Artists,* Spelman College Museum of Fine Art (1996).

Hassinger has served as visiting artist or artist in residence at the Studio Museum in Harlem, New York (1984–85); Brandywine Workshop, Philadelphia (1994); Rutgers University's Mason Gross School of the Arts, New Brunswick, New Jersey (1997); Randolph-Macon College, Lynchburg, Virginia (1997); MacDowell Colony, Peterborough, New Hampshire (2001); Nature Conservancy/Andy Warhol Estate, East Hampton, New York (2004); and Arcadia Summer Art Program (Kamp Kippy), Bar Harbor, Maine (2005). She is currently director of the Rinehart School of Sculpture at Maryland Institute College of Art.   [ACS]

PAMELA L. JENNINGS

(b. 1964, American; lives and works in Pittsburgh)

Pamela L. Jennings is a new-media artist, curator, writer, and educator. She received her BA in psychology from Oberlin College in 1986, MA in studio art from New York University and the International Center of Photography in 1990, and an MFA in computer arts from the School of Visual Arts, New York, in 1996. She also received a PhD in philosophy, computer science, and creative digital media from the Center for Advanced Inquiry in Integrative Arts in the School of Computer Science at the University of Plymouth, England, in 2006. Jennings serves as assistant professor of art and human computer interaction at Carnegie Mellon University.

Her digital media work integrates design, sound, text, sculpture, and video to produce interactive and conceptual pieces that engage issues of desire and communication within the subconscious. Exploring personal narratives and promoting public dialogue, Jennings uses technology to encourage communication, in the form of interactive games, in *Solitaire: dream journal* (1995). As a curator, she also investigates these themes in the exhibition *Speculative Data and the Creative Imaginary* (2007), sponsored by the Association for Computing Machinery's Creativity and Cognition Conference.

Jennings's new-media projects have been discussed in several texts, such as Lisa E. Farrington's *Creating Their Own Image: The History of African-American Women Artists*. As a new-media arts advocate, she has contributed to various publications, including *Felix: A Journal of Media Arts and Communication* and *Leonardo: Journal of the International Society for the Arts, Sciences and Technology*, and has completed commissioned research projects for both the Rockefeller Foundation and International Federation of Arts Councils and Culture Agencies. Jennings has received fellowships from the STUDIO for Creative Inquiry at Carnegie Mellon University, Pittsburgh; Banff Centre for the Arts, Alberta, Canada; Experimental Television Center, New York; and Women Make Movies, New York; among others. In New York, her work has been exhibited and screened at the Goethe-Institut, Joseph Papp Public Theater, Parsons School of Design, MIX: The New York Lesbian & Gay Experimental Film/Video Festival, Whitney Museum of American Art, Exit Art Gallery, and the Museum of Modern Art. She has also exhibited at Kiasma Museum of Contemporary Art, Helsinki; MIT, Cambridge, Massachusetts; and Cornell University, Ithaca, New York.   [MDH]

LAUREN KELLEY

(b. 1975, American; lives and works in Houston)

Lauren Kelley is an interdisciplinary artist. She has received a BFA from the Maryland Institute College of Art and an MFA from the School of the Art Institute of Chicago. She completed a residency at the Skowhegan School of Painting and Sculpture and is currently a resident at the Glassel School of Art's Core Artist-in-Residence Program at the Museum of Fine Arts, Houston.

Kelley uses the media of drawing, photography, sculpture, and video to critically explore ideas about black girl- and womanhood. Among the images and objects the artist makes are sculptural wigs composed of found objects and nontraditional materials, including candy, gum, and polyurethane resin, and black Barbie-like dolls to examine ideas on race and sexuality. Kelley's video, *Big Gurl* (2006), is a series of short, stop-animation videos that examine such real-life situations as body image, women's health, consumerism, and romantic relationships.

Kelley's work has appeared in many exhibitions—among them, *Project Row Houses, Round 12,* Project Row Houses, Houston (2000); *Wig Works,* DiverseWorks, Houston (2001); *YBW, Young Black Women,* Frick Lounge Gallery, Elmhurst College, Elmhurst, Illinois (2001); *Burnt,*

Fried, Pulled, Curled, Hyde Park Art Center, Chicago (2002); *Project: We Tell Tales,* Gallery 902, Chicago (2002); *Telling Our Story: The Art of YBW,* Prairie State College, Chicago Heights (2003); *Row Houses, Round 21 1/2,* Project Row Houses, Houston (2004); *Do-It-Yourself Art Fair,* Casket Factory, Dallas (2005); *Collect Them All! Soft Brown Narratives* and *Drawing Between the Lines,* Lawndale Art Center, Houston (2006); *Homage to Domestic Familiarity,* Anya Tish Gallery, Houston (2007); *Lone Star,* Museo de la Nación, Lima, Peru (2007); *Round 27: Race and Class,* Project Row Houses, Houston (2007); and *The Red Carpet Screening Room,* Rush Arts Gallery, Miami Design District (2007). Kelley is currently an instructor of art at Texas A & M University, Prairie View. [ACS]

YVETTE MATTERN
(b.1963, American; lives and works in Berlin)
Yvette Mattern, video artist and video designer of avant-garde opera, theater, and performance, received an MFA in screenwriting and directing at Columbia University. She has collaborated with many renowned artists, including video artist Vito Acconci, musician Don Byron, cinematographer Arthur Jafa, photographer Cindy Sherman, and writer Greg Tate.

Mattern created her first independent feature film, *Pearl,* in 1994, when she graduated from Columbia. She has used the medium of video art to examine personal experiences, identity, and cultural self-discovery. *The Zanzibar Project* (1998) reflects on her travel to Tanzania and Zanzibar in 1997, and her responses to female circumcision, misogyny, sexual tourism, postimperialism, magic, rituals, and her preconceived perceptions of African culture. Mattern's work is concerned with the study of the video grain and the painterly effects that it renders. She is also interested in the use and effect of light, the poetic word, and music in her installations, such as *Black Body Radiation* (2007). She further investigates the possibilities of light, text, music, and her mixed-race heritage in the text-based light-sculpture installation *Mulatta* (2007).

Her solo exhibitions include *Analog,* BALTIC Centre for Contemporary Art, Gateshead, England (2006), and *Video Box, White Box,* New York (2007). Among her group exhibitions are *Malcolm X, Man, Ideal, Icon,* Institute of Contemporary Art, Boston (1993); *Unpacking Europe,* Museum Boijmans Van Beuningen, Rotterdam (2001); *Just Passing Through,* Transmediale, Galerie BGF, Berlin (2003); *Peep Show,* Tribes Gallery, New York (2004); *Image Acts,* OfficeOps, Brooklyn (2005); *Everybody Wins,* Nuit Blanche Festival, Paris (2006); *You Won't Feel a Thing: On Panic, Obsession, Rituality and Anesthesia,* WYSPA Institute of Art, Gdansk, Poland (2007); *Black Light/White Noise: Light and Sound in Contemporary Art,* Contemporary Arts Museum Houston (2007); and *Equatorial Rhythms,* Sternersen Museum, Oslo (2007).

Mattern has served as artist in residence at the BALTIC Centre for Contemporary Art, Gateshead, England (2005–6), and is currently artist in residence at the Center for Contemporary Art, Ujazdowski Castle, Warsaw (2007). [ACS]

BRADLEY MCCALLUM AND JACQUELINE TARRY
(b. 1966, b. 1964, American; live and work in Brooklyn, and maintain a studio in Beijing)
Bradley McCallum and Jacqueline Tarry began collaborating in 1998. McCallum received his BFA in sculpture from Virginia Commonwealth University, in 1989, and completed his MFA at Yale University. Tarry received her BA in philosophy from the State University of New York, Buffalo, and participated in the Whitney Museum of American Art's Independent Study Program in 2003. McCallum and Tarry have been commissioned to complete a memorial for Malcolm X at the intersection of Central Park and Malcolm X Boulevard, in New York.

Their photographs, large-scale public projects, performances, and installations focus on their experiences as an interracial couple. Since their initial collaboration, *Witness: Perspectives on Police Violence,* McCallum and Tarry have challenged audiences to confront not just the issues of race and social injustice in communities but the historical precedents that continue to impede the progress of equality in contemporary society. Traveling nationally and globally, McCallum and Tarry have tackled such politically charged topics as homelessness, police brutality, and the institution of slavery. Defining their process as performative sculpture, McCallum and Tarry's seminal works seek to give voice to marginalized groups—the witnesses and victims of gun violence in *Manhole Cover Project: A Gun Legacy* (1996) and the homeless youth of Seattle in *Endurance* (2003). Their featured video *Cut* (2006) is an emotionally charged self-portrait.

McCallum and Tarry have exhibited at such New York venues as the Bronx Museum of the Arts, New York Public Library, Lower Manhattan Cultural Council, White Columns, Socrates Sculpture Park, Marvelli Gallery, Rush Arts Gallery, and Nathan Cummings Foundation; Neuberger Museum of Art, Purchase, New York; Wadsworth Atheneum Museum, Hartford, Conn.; Aljira, a Center for Contemporary Art, Newark, New Jersey; Nichido Contemporary Art Gallery and Tokyo Wonder Site, Tokyo; and Conner Contemporary Art, Washington, D.C.   [MDH]

BARBARA MCCULLOUGH

(b. 1947, American; lives and works in Los Angeles)

Barbara McCullough, a veteran of the film industry, earned a BFA in mass communications and an MFA in theater arts from the University of California, Los Angeles. Considered one of the first pioneering African American experimental filmmakers, her work has spanned commercial, independent, and public television productions. Commercially,

she has worked as the digital, special, and visual effects production manager on such films as *Made in Heaven* (1987), *Toys* (1992), *The Color of Night* (1994), *Ace Ventura: When Nature Calls* (1995), and *The Nutty Professor* (1996).

McCullough's work has been shown at film festivals and in museums throughout the country. Influenced by folklorist and writer Zora Neale Hurston, she creates films that reflect the diversity and universality of the black experience. Among her experimental titles are *Water Ritual #1: An Urban Rite of Purification* (1979), *Shopping Bag Spirits and Freeway Fetishes: Reflections on Ritual Space* (1980), and *Fragments* (1980). The films examine African diasporic cultural continuity, the importance and use of ritual in the work of black artists, and the means of ritual as an act of purification and catharsis. *World Saxophone Quartet* (1980), about the innovative jazz saxophonists Hamiet Bluiet, Oliver Lake, Julius Hemphill, and David Murray, is McCullough's only film to be shown on PBS.

In 1980, McCullough and filmmaker Julie Dash hosted a special screening of work by black independent filmmakers at the Cannes Film Festival. This seminal screening introduced the filmmakers to the industry and initiated a market of black independent films. Barbara McCullough is currently the manager of recruitment at Rhythm & Hues Studios, and is committed to providing opportunities for black filmmakers and producers.   [ACS]

TRACEY MOFFATT

(b. 1960, Australian; lives and works in New York)

Tracey Moffatt, an Australian artist of Aboriginal descent, received a degree in visual communications from Queensland College of Art, Brisbane. She first garnered critical attention in 1989 for *Something More,* a photographic series that explores issues of history, race, representation, and sexuality.

Although raised by white foster parents, Moffatt's Aboriginal background informs the investigation of racial differences in her work. She uses film, photography, and video to examine childhood, memory, popular culture, and the histories of art, cinema, and photography. She explores constructions of identity in her film- and video-based work by employing stylized stage settings and nonrealistic scenarios, in such early pieces as *Nice Coloured Girls* (1987) and *Night Cries: A Rural Tragedy* (1989). The recent photographic series—*Fourth* (2001), *Adventure Series* (2004), and *Under the Sign of Scorpio* (2005)—take on fame and celebrity.

Moffatt's oeuvre has been the subject of recent solo international exhibitions: *Portraits* and *Doomed* (a collaboration with artist Gary Hillberg), Roslyn Oxley 9 Gallery, Sydney (2007); *Between Dreams and Reality,* Spazio Oberdan, Milan and Montreal (2006); *Love and Adventures,* Steven Kasher Gallery, New York (2006); *Under the Sign of Scorpio,* Roslyn Oxley 9 Gallery, Sydney (2005); *Fourth,* Bendigo Art Gallery, Victoria (2005); her first retrospective, Museum of Contemporary Art, Sydney (December 2003–4); and her first United States exhibition, *Free-Falling,* Dia Center for the Arts, New York (1997).

Tracey Moffatt has been featured in many group exhibitions: *Nan Goldin, Cindy Sherman, Tracey Moffatt, Barbara Kruger,* New Art Gallery, Walsall, England (2003); *The Disembodied Spirit,* Kemper Museum of Contemporary Art, Kansas City, Kansas (2004); *Only Skin Deep: Changing Visions of the American Self,* International Center of Photography, New York (2004); *Minority Report: Challenging Intolerance in Contemporary Denmark,* Aarhus Festival of Contemporary Art (2004); *The Difference Between You and Me,* Ian Potter Museum of Art, University of Melbourne (2005); *Once Upon a Time Walt Disney,* Galeries Nationales du Grand Palais, Paris (2006) and Montreal Museum of Fine Arts (2007); *Concept: Photography—Dialogues and Attitudes, From the Traditional Forms of Photography to Auteur Photography,* Ludwig Museum—Museum of Contemporary Art, Budapest (2007); and *Supercharged: The Car in Contemporary Culture,* Institute of Modern Art, Brisbane (touring exhibition, 2006–8).

Her work has appeared in such important international exhibitions as the Kwangju Biennale, Korea (1995), São Paolo Biennale, Brazil (1997), and the 47th Venice Biennale (1997), and her films have been screened at the Cannes Film Festival (1990 and 1993).   [ACS]

WANGECHI MUTU
(b. 1972, Kenyan; lives and works in New York)
Wangechi Mutu, as she investigates the lives and bodies of women, is consistently lauded for her innovative use of media. Trained as both anthropologist and sculptor, she received her BFA from Cooper Union for the Advancement of Science and Art, New York, in 1996, and her MFA from the School of Sculpture at Yale University in 2000.

Employing techniques from various media—collage, installation, performance, sculpture, and video—Mutu's work explores the aftermath of cultural and physical devastation on the body. She is primarily recognized for her large-scale collages on Mylar, in which she takes magazine imagery from fashion publications, *National Geographic,* and porn magazines and conflates the selections with found objects and hand-drawn and painted surfaces. In this way, she creates bodies of work that merge the beautiful with the grotesque and the barren with abundance, as she attempts to construct an alternative narrative seeping in new mythologies. These heavily collaged renderings subsequently produce elaborate figures that present a visual vocabulary of pleasure, pain, war, colonialism, high fashion, fertility, and, ultimately, survival.

In Wangechi Mutu's return to video and performance art, she continues to explore the black female body. Such works as *Cutting* (2004) and *Amazing Grace* (2005) are rife with political conflict and ambiguity of origin and place. *Cutting* presents the artist's silhouetted figure hacking feverishly at a piece of wood with a machete. *Amazing Grace,* which contemplates the slave trade and its connection to water, speaks to migration, diasporic connections, and the remarkable aspects of survival.

Mutu has had solo exhibitions at the Miami Art Museum and San Francisco Museum of Modern Art, among others. She has also participated in numerous group shows: PKM Gallery, Beijing; the Elizabeth A. Sackler Center for Feminist Art, Brooklyn Museum; Michael Stevenson Gallery, Cape Town; Santa Fe Biennial, New Mexico; Royal Academy of the Arts, London; in Seville, 2nd Biennial of Contemporary Art, and Centro Andaluz de Arte Contemporaneo; New Museum of Contemporary Art and Rush Arts Gallery, New York; and 2nd Johannesburg Biennale, to name a few. Mutu's work appears in the collections of the Museum of Modern Art, Whitney Museum of American Art, and Studio Museum in Harlem, New York; Museum of Contemporary Art, Chicago; and Museum of Contemporary Art, Los Angeles.   [M D H]

SENGA NENGUDI
(b. 1943, American; lives and works in Colorado Springs, Colorado)
Senga Nengudi, a mixed-media artist widely recognized for sculptural and installation work, engages issues of body and movement and comments on transitory media and everyday objects. She received both her BA in art and MA in sculpture from California State University, Los Angeles, in 1966 and 1971, respectively.

Nengudi garnered mainstream attention in the 1970s for the inclusion of traditional African motifs, Eastern philosophy, and ritual practices in her minimalist installations. Her readily recognizable media—sand, rocks, and nylon stockings—provide an accessibility for understanding complex themes of spirituality, transformation, womanhood, and memory. Many of her installations are site specific, occupying gallery space where sheer nylon mesh, filled with sand, is interwoven into stylized compositions that suggest hyperbolic movements of the arms and legs. The nylon material, which has been knotted, stretched, and filled, also comments upon the daily lives of women—a metaphor for survival when adjusting to inaccessible standards of beauty and transformation because of pregnancy, scarring, and domestic violence. Nengudi's tenure as an artist in residence at the Fabric Workshop and Museum produced her first video-based works, *Warp Trance* (2007) and *The Threader* (2007). Inspired by Pennsylvania's textile mills, *Warp Trance* and *The Threader* merge sound and video to communicate the repetitive composition in a work that incorporates ritual and movement.

Nengudi's installation, video, and performance work has also been included in numerous group and solo exhibitions: *Out of Action: Between Performance and Object, 1949–1979* (1998), *Clothesline: Art, Clothing, Identity* (2005), *Double Consciousness: Black Conceptual Art Since 1970* (2005), and *WACK! Art and the Feminist Revolution* (2007), among many others. She has been the recipient of numerous awards, including a Louis Comfort Tiffany Foundation Award, Anonymous Was A Woman, and New York State Council on the Arts grant. Her work appears in such collections as the Museum of Contemporary Art, Los Angeles; Studio Museum in Harlem, New York; and Carnegie Museum of Art, Pittsburgh. Nengudi currently teaches at the University of Colorado, Colorado Springs.   [M D H]

MICHELLE DENISE PARKERSON
(b. 1955, American; lives and works in Philadelphia, Pa.)
Michelle Denise Parkerson is an independent filmmaker, producer, video artist, poet, writer, lecturer, entrepreneur, and activist. She received her BA in communications from Temple University in 1974. The founder of Eye of the Storm, a Washington, D.C.–based production company, she

also serves as an assistant professor in film and media arts in the School of Communications and Theater at Temple.

As an undergraduate, Parkerson's films were received with critical acclaim, but it was her work in public television that introduced her films to a larger audience. Her documentaries *But Then, She's Betty Carter* (1980) and *Gotta Make This Journey: Sweet Honey in the Rock* (1983) primarily investigate the aspects of race and gender in narratives by and about African American women. Parkerson intensified her commitment to presenting diverse images of African American gays and lesbians on film with her intimate portrait of male impersonator Stormé DeLarverie in *Stormé: The Lady of the Jewel Box* (1987); a futuristic account of the New World Order in *Odds and Ends* (1993); and a collaborative tribute, with Ada Gay Griffin, director of Third World Newsreel, to activist and writer Audre Lorde in *A Litany for Survival: The Life and Work of Audre Lorde* (1995). These films further cemented her position as a pioneer in the genre.

Parkerson's films have been screened nationwide on public television and at numerous festivals, such as the Sundance Film Festival and San Francisco International Film Festival, where she took both Audience and Best Biography awards. She has received grants and fellowships from the Rockefeller Foundation, Corporation for Public Broadcasting, and American Film Institute, among others. An educator, Parkerson has held professorships and lectured at many academic institutions, including Yale University, Harvard University, the Institute for Policy Studies, Howard University, and Northwestern University. She has also presented work at the Museum of Modern Art, New York; National Film Board of Canada; Walker Art Center, Minneapolis; and National Black Arts Festival, Atlanta. [MDH]

JESSICA ANN PEAVY
(b. 1982, American; lives and works in New York)
Jessica Ann Peavy creates multichannel works that comment on the social and psychological states of young, urban African American women. She received her BFA in film and television from the Tisch School of the Arts, New York University, in 2004, and completed her MFA in photography, video, and related media at the School of Visual Arts the same year.

A conceptual multidisciplinary artist with a background in film-making, Jessica Ann Peavy moves seamlessly between photography, installation, performance, and video, offering meditations on woman-hood in an ever-changing cultural landscape. Simultaneously presenting the role of the video vixen, social commentator and climber, vigilante and self-reflexive Jane Doe, Peavy's characters offer intimate, and often-times comic, perspectives on success, beauty, assimilation, and popular culture. Her acknowledgment of the black female body as a subject of inquiry, desire, and envy leads her to construct narratives that consider the complexities of the body politic in the contemporary age.

Peavy has exhibited at the Brooklyn Museum, Brooklyn Arts Council, Rush Arts Gallery, and DUMBO Arts Festival, in New York; Artformz Alternative, in Miami; and the Black Floor Gallery, in Philadelphia. She has participated in performances, programs, and residencies at Franklin Furnace Fund for Performance Art, Performa 07, Tribeca Film Festival Artists Awards Program, and the 2007 Smack Mellon Arts Studio Program, in New York. Her films have been featured in festivals in New York, Los Angeles, and London, and she has received the Warner Bros. Pictures Film Producing grant and an Aaron Siskind grant. [MDH]

HOWARDENA PINDELL

(b. 1943, American; lives and works in New York)

Howardena Pindell received her BFA with honors from Boston University in 1965 and MFA from Yale University in 1967. She is a pioneering mixed-media artist, educator, writer, critic, and curator who initially garnered international attention in the 1960s and '70s for her abstract painting and sculpture; later, in 1980, she began experimenting with video. From 1967 to 1978, Pindell worked at the Museum of Modern Art, New York, stepping up periodically into positions of greater responsibility, until 1978, when she accepted the position of associate professor at the State University of New York, Stony Brook.

Throughout her career, Pindell has created works that are committed to human rights and the essential leanings of feminism. As a founding member of the Artist-in-Residence Gallery, one of the first feminist galleries in New York, she addressed issues of poverty, racism, and gender oppression. Emerging from a select group of African American artists who worked in abstraction in the 1960s, Pindell grew more interested in relational space. Her leaning toward collage and the addition of three-dimensional media resulted from considering the artmaking process as physical and metaphorical meditations on deconstruction. Never abandoning these motifs, merely adding to them, Pindell's video and performance work addresses issues of identity germane to the black woman. Her iconic video piece *Free, White and 21* (1980) confronts issues of skin color and racism as she assumes the roles of the multiple characters that make up this arresting narrative.

Pindell's work has been included in numerous exhibitions, nationally and internationally: in New York, at the Metropolitan Museum of Art, Museum of Modern Art, Whitney Museum of American Art, Studio Museum in Harlem, P.S. 1, and Jamaica Arts Center; in London, the Institute of Contemporary Art; in Washington, D.C., the National Portrait Gallery and the Smithsonian Institution; and in Brazil, the São Paulo Biennale, among many others. She has been awarded a National Endowment for the Arts Award and the Most Distinguished Body of Work or Performance Award from the College Art Association. Her work appears in many public and private collections: in New York, the Brooklyn Museum, The Kitchen, Museum of Modern Art, New York Public Library, and New Museum of Contemporary Art; in Atlanta, High Museum of Art; Museum of Contemporary Art, Chicago; Philadelphia Museum of Art; and in Washington, D.C., National Gallery of Art.   [MDH]

ADRIAN PIPER

(b. 1948, American; lives and works in Berlin)

Adrian Margaret Smith Piper, a first-generation conceptual artist, art theorist, and philosopher, received an AA in Fine Arts from the School of Visual Arts, New York (1969), BA in Philosophy from City College of New York (1974), and PhD in Philosophy from Harvard University (1981). She also studied at the University of Heidelberg, Germany, in 1977–78.

Piper uses a variety of media, including photography, performance, drawing, video, and installation, to create works that excavate, examine, and challenge such highly charged issues as identity, racism, society, and xenophobia. She often interjects herself into her work to act as a mediator between the artwork and the viewer. The work often unsettles viewers by forcing them to confront their racial prejudices and preconceptions.

A renowned philosopher and art theorist, Piper has been particularly influenced by Kant and his writings on aesthetic judgment. Her two-volume book *Out of Order, Out of Sight: Selected Writings in Meta-Art, 1968–1992* (1996) chronicles the development of her thinking about her artwork and the mainstream art world, and her growing awareness of herself as a creative, racial, and gendered subject situated in an often marginalized cultural and social context.

Piper has been awarded fellowships from many institutions: the National Endowment for the Arts, Guggenheim Memorial Foundation, New York State Council on the Arts, National Endowment for the Humanities, Andrew Mellon Foundation, Woodrow Wilson Foundation, and the Institute for Advanced Study, known as Wissenschaftskolleg zu Berlin. Her awards and honors include honorary doctorate degrees from the California Institute of the Arts (1992) and the Massachusetts College of Art (1994), the Skowhegan Medal for Sculptural Installation (1995), and the New York Dance & Performance Award (the Bessie) for Installation & New Media (2001).

She has participated in seminal exhibitions, including *Concept Art,* Städtisches Museum, Leverkusen, Germany (1969); *Information,* Museum of Modern Art, New York (1970); *Art as a Verb,* Maryland Institute College of Art (1988), and *Double Consciousness: Black Conceptual Art Since 1970,* Contemporary Arts Musum Houston (2005). Two simultaneous retrospective exhibitions, *Adrian Piper: A Retrospective* and *MEDI(t) Ations: Adrian Piper's Videos, Installations, Performances and Soundworks 1968–1992,* traveled in the United States in 2000 and 2001. Her work is represented in important private and public collections both nationally and internationally.   [ACS]

TRACEY ROSE

(b. 1974, South African; lives and works in Johannesburg and Durban, and in London)

Tracey Rose is widely recognized for her multichannel video works, photographs, and performances that investigate questions of gender, sexuality, and race. She received her BFA with honors from the University of the Witwatersrand, Johannesburg, in 1996, and her MFA from Goldsmiths College, London, in 2007. She has participated in residencies at the Khoj International Artists Workshop, Vasind, India; South African National Gallery, Cape Town; ArtPace, San Antonio; Hollywood Hills Horrorhouse, Los Angeles; London School of Hygiene and Tropical Medicine; and OK Centrum, Linz, Austria.

Rose's video and performance work often reflects the rapidly evolving societies in South Africa and beyond. Her employment of new media problematizes the role of the artist and muse by presenting herself as subject and object, with the assistance of costumes, found objects, and props. Rose's earlier work has tackled issues of race and gender through such visual conceits as her body and hair. By making her own body a site of investigation, she uses it as a locus of artistic representation and of gendered constructions of identity. Her other works have confronted such issues as cultural authenticity, legitimacy, labor, and visual iconography.

Tracey Rose has exhibited nationally and internationally, and has participated in solo exhibitions at The Project, New York; Düsseldorf Art Fair; Moderna Museet, Stockholm; Goodman Gallery, Johannesburg; and Le Studio–Yvon Lambert, Paris. She has also been included in group exhibitions at Center de Cultura Contemporània de Barcelona; 52nd Venice Biennale; Brooklyn Museum, International Center of Photography, New Museum of Contemporary Art, and the Studio Museum in Harlem, in New York; Museum of Contemporary Art, Los Angeles; Haywood Gallery, London; Centre Georges Pompidou, Paris; Johannesburg Art Gallery; and the Bard College Center for Curatorial Studies, Annandale-on-Hudson, New York. Her work has been screened at the 19th Worldwide Video Festival, Amsterdam, and has appeared in the Stockholm Art Fair (2000), Dak'Art 2000, Dakar Biennale, Senegal, and 2nd Johannesburg Biennale. She has conducted live performances at such artistic venues as the Brooklyn Museum, New York; Goldsmiths College and Tate Modern, London; La Panderia, Mexico City; and Rensselaer Polytechnic Institute, Troy, New York.   [MDH]

EVE SANDLER

(b. 1957, American; lives and works in New York)

Eve Sandler is an artist who uses a variety of media—installation, jewelry design, metalsmithing, painting, sculpture, and video—to explore black female identity, culture, memory, ritual, and the sacred. She has exhibited her artwork internationally at such museums as the Smithsonian Institution; Frans Hals Museum, Haarlem, Netherlands; Studio Museum in Harlem, New York; and New Orleans Museum of Art. Her work has been profiled in the *International Review of African American Art* (1990) and *Gumbo Ya-Ya: An Anthology of Contemporary African American Women Artists* (1995). Sandler served as artist in residence at the Studio Museum in Harlem (1990–91) and has received numerous grants and awards for her work, including a New York Foundation for the Arts Fellowship for Video and Distribution grant.

Among the exhibitions in which she has been featured are: *Free Expressions,* Center for the Arts, Mount Vernon, New York (1985); *Of the Spirit,* Pittsburgh Center for the Arts (1996); *Postcards from Black America,* De Beyerd Museum, Amsterdam (1998); *Resonant Forms: Contemporary African American Women Sculptors,* Anacostia Museum and Center for African American History and Culture, Smithsonian Institution, Washington, D.C. (1999); *Soothsayers: She Who Speaks the Truth,* Painted Bride Art Center, Philadelphia (1999); *Merging of the Crossroads,* Pittsburgh Center for the Arts (1999); *The Garment Magical,* Skylight Gallery, Bedford Stuyvesant Restoration Corporation, Brooklyn (2003); *Living with Art: Modern and Contemporary African American Art from the Collection of Alitash Kebede,* Museum of Texas Tech University, Lubbock (2003); and *Border Crossing: Artists from the Mary H. Dana Women Artists Series,* Mabel Smith Douglass Library, Rutgers University, New Brunswick, New Jersey (2004).

Sandler's autobiographical works, which employ personal narratives, increasingly use the moving video to reveal, confront, and heal what is buried, silenced, and most painful in society. She creates compelling installation environments and video works of astonishing beauty and mystery that disturb yet draw in viewers, so that they cannot distance themselves from the unfolding—and often unsettling—drama that lies beneath the surface. Her painterly vision can be seen in her first foray into video, *The Wash: A Cleaning Story* (1999). It intimately explores both the artist's body and memory for scars and the emotional remnants of childhood sexual abuse in her family—and in black communities at large. Subsequent works have explored her rich multicultural heritage, complex family history, and the family secrets that dwell therein.   [ACS]

BERNI SEARLE

(b. 1964, South African; lives and works in Cape Town)

Berni Searle, a South African artist, received a BA and MFA at the Michaelis School of Fine Art, University of Cape Town. Before the abolition of apartheid, she was classified as *coloured,* a median category created for people of mixed racial descent. Searle employs a variety of media, such as photography, film, and video, to challenge the conditions and repercussions of apartheid, to address racial and gender inequities, and to posit ongoing explorations of history, memory, and place. Her first video work, *Snow White* (2001), premiered at the 49th Venice Biennale (2001); the artist has been incorporating video into her work ever since, including *A Matter of Time* (2003), *Home and Away* (2003), *Vapor* (2004), *About to Forget* (2005), and *Alibama* (2006–7).

Searle's work has been the subject of many solo exhibitions: *Colour Matters,* Kunsthalle Stadtgallerie, Osnabrück, Germany (2001); *MATRIX: A Matter of Time,* Berkeley Art Museum and Pacific Film Archive, Berkeley, California (2003); *The Space Between: Artists Engaging Race and*

Syncretism, Davis Museum and Cultural Center, Wellesley College (2003); *Home and Away,* NMAC Montenmedio Arte Contemporaneo, Vejer de la Frontera, Spain (2003); *Float* (as the Standard Bank Young Artist for Visual Art), at Grahamstown, Cape Town, and Johannesburg (2003–4); *To love, to fear, to leave,* screening, Performa05, New York (2005); *Berni Searle: Video Works,* BildMuseet, Umeå, Sweden (2005); *Presence,* Speed Museum, Louisville, Kentucky (2005); and *Approach,* Contemporary Art Museum, Institute for Research in Art, at the University of South Florida, Tampa, and the Krannert Art Museum, University of Illinois, Urbana-Champaign (2007).

Berni Searle has participated in many international exhibitions, including *Life's Little Necessities,* 2nd Johannesburg Biennale (1997); 7th International Cairo Biennale (1998); *Portrat Afrika,* House of World Cultures, Berlin (2000); *Authentic/Ex-centric,* 49th Venice Biennale (2001); *Power and Poetics in Contemporary South African Art,* Cathedral of St. John the Divine and the Museum for African Art, New York (2004); *Always a Little Further,* 51st Venice Biennale (2005); *TEXTures: Word and Symbol in Contemporary African Art,* Smithsonian National Museum of African Art, Washington, D.C. (2005); 7th Dakar Biennale, Senegal (2006); and *New Photography 2007,* Museum of Modern Art, New York.

Searle is the recipient of many awards and residencies: UNESCO award, 7th International Cairo Biennale (1998); residency, Gasworks, London (2000); DaimlerChrysler Award for South African Contemporary Art (2000); Civitella Ranieri Fellowship, Umbria (2001); Ministry of Culture Prize, Dak'Art 2000, Dakar Biennale, Senegal; and Standard Bank Young Artist for Visual Art (2003). Her work is featured in the traveling exhibitions *Global Feminisms* (2007), *Darkroom: Photography and New Media in South Africa 1950–Present* (2007–9), and *Black Womanhood: Images, Icons, and Ideologies of the African Body* (2008–9). [ACS]

XAVIERA SIMMONS

(b. 1974, American; lives and works in Brooklyn, N.Y.)

Xaviera Simmons is a multidisciplinary artist whose emphasis is on photography, video, and performance-based work. She received her BFA in photography from Bard College in 2004 and participated in the Independent Study Program of the Whitney Museum of American Art in 2005.

Simmons is particularly interested in exploring the making of art as an inclusive and collaborative practice. In her most recent work, she engages music, visual culture, and space by creating installation-based work equipped with video and sound components, which are visible and, in many instances, audible outside the exhibition area itself. When she uses these elements, environments become activated and affect the ways in which sounds are processed and remembered by the viewer; the selection of these songs can potentially inform and incite social and political responses. She also contemplates blackface performance, urban and suburban culture, and the black female body in her work.

Solo exhibition venues include the Contemporary Arts Museum Houston; Santa Barbara Contemporary Arts Forum, California; Real Art Ways, Hartford, Connecticut; and Jamaica Center for Arts and Learning and Art in General, New York. She has also exhibited at the Studio Museum in Harlem and Saatchi and Saatchi, New York; Zacheta National Gallery of Art, Warsaw; and Context Galleries, Derry, Ireland. Simmons has also received awards from and participated in residencies and fellowships at, among others, the New Museum of Contemporary Art, Lower Manhattan Cultural Council, and Art in General, in New York; Center for Photography, Woodstock, New York; and Platform Garanti Contemporary Art Center, Istanbul. She is the 2008 recipient of the David C. Driskell Prize. [MDH]

LORNA SIMPSON

(b. 1960, American; lives and works in Brooklyn, N.Y.)

Lorna Simpson is known for confronting and challenging conventional views of gender, identity, culture, history, and memory with large-scale photograph and text works that are formally elegant and subtly provocative. The Brooklyn-based artist received a BFA in photography from the School of Visual Arts, New York, and an MFA in visual arts from the University of California, San Diego.

Simpson confronts and critiques the ethnographic and social classification purposes of nineteenth-century documentary photography. Her early work embodies images and issues involving the black woman: her social position, her invisibility, and the objectification she must face as the recipient of the dominant male gaze. Simpson has often focused on the figure, shown either faceless or with body cropped, combined with fragments of text that confound the viewer's expectations of narrative and identity. Since 1997, she has created video installations that expand on her previous explorations of social and interpersonal issues while opening new directions in nonnarrative experimental film.

Simpson's work has been featured in solo exhibitions, including *Lorna Simpson: Matrix 107*, Wadsworth Atheneum Museum, Hartford, Conn. (1989); *Lorna Simpson: Projects 23*, Museum of Modern Art, New York (1990); *Lorna Simpson: Interior/Exterior, Full/Empty*, Wexner Center for the Arts, Ohio State University (1997); *Lorna Simpson*, Studio Museum in Harlem, New York (2002); *Scenarios: Recent Work by Lorna Simpson* (1999–2001, traveling exhibition); and a midcareer survey organized by the American Federation of the Arts (2007, traveling).

Among the seminal group exhibitions in which Simpson's work has been presented are the Whitney Biennial, Whitney Museum of American Art, New York (1991, 1993, 2002); *Black Male: Representations of Masculinity in Contemporary American Art*, Whitney Museum of American Art, New York (1994); *Bearing Witness: Contemporary Works by African American Women Artists* (1996, traveling exhibition); *Trade Routes: History and Geography: Life's Little Necessities: Installations by Women in the 1990s*, 2nd Johannesburg Biennale (1997); *The American Century: Art and Culture, 1950–2000*, Whitney Museum of American Art, New York (1999); *Reflections in Black: A History of Black Photographers, 1840 to the Present*, Anacostia Museum and Center for African American History and Culture, Smithsonian Institution, Washington, D.C. (2000); *Documenta XI*, Kassel, Germany (2002); and *Only Skin Deep: Changing Visions of the American Self*, International Center for Photography, New York (2003). [ACS]

CAULEEN SMITH

(b. 1967, American; lives and works in Boston, Mass.)

Cauleen Smith is a prolific multimedia artist who creates films, art installations, and experimental videos. She received a BA from San Francisco State University's School of Creative Arts and an MFA from the School of Theater-Television-Film, University of California, Los Angeles. In her mission to disrupt clichéd depictions of African Americans, Smith has created works that extend the genre of science fiction to include futuristic concepts of blackness as well as the overwhelming and unshakable vestiges of isolationism and displacement. She also examines deeply embedded cultural assumptions and provides insights into the consequences that may result.

Smith is best known for her feature film debut, *Drylongso* (1998), about a young woman who uses a Polaroid camera to document the existence of young black men: She thinks they are an endangered species. The film received critical attention and numerous awards at the Hamptons Film Festival (1998), Urbanworld Film Festival (2000), and Los Angeles Pan-African Film Festival (2000), and Smith was honored with the Movado Someone to Watch Award at the Independent Spirit Awards (2000). Her films have been presented at Yerba Buena Center for the Arts's Inaugural Exhibition, San Francisco (1993); *Race in Digital Space* (2001); the international Afrofuturist exhibition *Black to the Future,* at the Cinema de Baile, Amsterdam (2004); and *You Wear It Well—Short Films and Videos about Fashion and Beauty Around the World,* Cinespace, Los Angeles (2006).

She has collaborated with poet A. Van Jordan to create *I Want to See My Skirt,* a multichannel video with 3D installation that investigates the photographs of Malian photographer Malick Sidibé and the construction of identity through style and created images. *I Want to See My Skirt* was shown at the Fluent-Collaborative test site, Austin, Texas, in 2006. Smith's recent multimedia installation, *NTSC* (2007), at Women and Their Work Gallery, Austin, incorporates drawing, sculpture, and video to investigate cultural assumptions and the regulation of media.

She is currently collaborating with the New York–based experimental art operative Creative Time to create a short film in conjunction with artist Paul Chan's production of the play *Waiting for Godot* in New Orleans. The film, utilizing both fantasy and documentation, explores the theme of waiting, as it relates to New Orleanians and their dogged determination to rehabilitate their Hurricane Katrina–ravaged homes. In 2008, Smith was awarded a prestigious film/video grant from Creative Capital.   [ACS]

PAMELA PHATSIMO SUNSTRUM

(b. 1980, South African; lives and works in Baltimore)
Pamela Phatsimo Sunstrum received her MFA from Mount Royal School of Art, Maryland Institute College of Art, in 2007. She received an undergraduate degree at the University of North Carolina, Chapel Hill, and has traveled extensively in Africa and Asia. While enrolled at the University of North Carolina, Sunstrum served as an artist in residence at El Taller Portobelo, an artists' collective–organized art colony, based in Panama, that focuses on the arts of the African Diaspora in general and the area's indigenous arts in particular. Recently, Sunstrum participated in the Skowhegan School of Painting and Sculpture Summer Residency Program.

A new-media artist, whose digital photo animation alludes to histories that are ancestral and archaeological, Sunstrum takes stories and blurs them with other stories that, in their urgency and immediacy, conjure impending moments. Alluding to her personal experience and extensive travel, Sunstrum's work references migration, nationhood, and identity. In further meditations on identity, she advances the dialogue of a deconstructed and hyphened self as she uses digital fragments and repetition. Interested in the body as a theme and point of entry, she explains that "[b]odies, as figures, in my work become whispering coconspirators busy at the task of defacing dominant histories while themselves refusing to be obliterated, removed, or otherwise worked over."

Her work has appeared at the Maryland Institute College of Art; Artspace, Raleigh, North Carolina; Diaspora Vibe Gallery, Miami; and Vaknin Gallery, Atlanta. In 2007, she participated in the 4th Annual Transmodern Festival, Baltimore.   [MDH]

JOCELYN TAYLOR

(b. 1962, American; lives and works in Castaic, California)
Jocelyn Taylor is a video artist, activist, filmmaker, and writer. She received an MFA from the California Institute of the Arts, Valencia, and completed the Independent Study Program at the Whitney Museum of American Art, New York.

Taylor began working with video in 1989 while a member of ACT-UP (AIDS Coalition to Unleash Power). Her subsequent films *Be a Diva*

(1990) and *Like a Prayer* (1991) illustrate the importance of the medium as a tool for activism. She has been a member of several media activist groups, including DIVA-TV (an affinity group of ACT-UP), House of Color (a video collective of people of color), and the public access television station DYKE-TV.

Her autobiographical *Father Knows Best* (1990) and *Frankie & Jocie* (1994) examine the complex family relationships that have developed because of her sexual orientation. She is best known for the works that explore sexuality. The video installation and film *Bodily Functions* (1995) and *Jocelyn Taylor's Erotica* (1996), which was a featured segment on the popular HBO series *Real Sex,* examine issues of body image, sexuality, gender, and the erotic body

Jocelyn Taylor's work has been presented in such solo exhibitions as *Alien at Rest,* Deitch Projects, New York (1996), and *Bodies of Work and Residues of Hand Gestures,* University of Milwaukee Art Museum (1997). She was commissioned by the New York City Public Art Fund to participate in its program *In the Public Realm.* Her video installation *A Story of Color* (2000) was on view at two sites in New York. Taylor was also selected to create a work for *Artists Create for the New Millennium,* a project funded by the National Endowment for the Arts and the Mid-Atlantic Arts Foundation (2000). In addition, she served as artist in residence at Art-In-General, New York (1996), Art Center South Florida, Miami Beach (1997), and the California Institute of the Arts, Valencia (2004).

Taylor participated in the exhibitions *Life's Little Necessities,* 2nd Johannesburg Biennale, and *The Gaze,* Momenta Art, New York, in 1997. Her films have been featured in festivals and exhibitions in New York, Los Angeles, Havana, Minneapolis, Venezuela, Canada, France, and the Netherlands. [ACS]

KARA WALKER

(b. 1969, American; lives and works in New York)

Kara Walker earned a BFA from the Atlanta College of Art and an MFA, in Painting and Printmaking, from the Rhode Island School of Design. In 1997, she made history when, at twenty-seven, she received the John D. and Catherine T. MacArthur Foundation Achievement grant. She is also the recipient of the Deutsche Bank Prize (2004), the Lucelia Artist Award from the Smithsonian American Art Museum (2004), and the Larry Aldrich Award (2005).

Walker uses cut-paper silhouettes, drawings, paintings, performances, and videos to examine history, race, and sexuality. Her highly charged works focus on complicated, sometimes controversial, themes: power relationships between slaves and slave owners, sexual perversities, violence, race, class, sexuality, and the Jim Crow South. Her 2004 video *Testimony: Narrative of a Negress Burdened by Good Intentions* is the artist's foray into the medium. Her subsequent video-based works challenge and usurp romanticized notions of the antebellum South as portrayed in Harriet Beecher Stowe's 1852 antislavery novel *Uncle Tom's Cabin,* the 1939 Academy Award–winning *Gone with the Wind,* and the 1946 Walt Disney film *Song of the South.*

Her work has been presented in seminal exhibitions, including the Whitney Biennial, Whitney Museum of American Art, New York (1997, 2006); *Re/Righting History: Counternarratives by Contemporary African-American Artists,* Katonah Museum of Art, New York (1999); *Looking Forward, Looking Black,* Elaine L. Jacob Gallery, Wayne State University, Detroit (1999); Site Santa Fe's Fifth International Biennial, New Mexico (2004–5); *Legacies: Contemporary Artists Reflect on Slavery,* New-York Historical Society (2006–7); and the touring exhibition *Global Feminisms* (2007).

Walker's work has been the subject of several solo exhibitions, among them *Presenting Negro Scenes Drawn Upon My Passage Through the South and Reconfigured for the Benefit of Enlightened Audiences Wherever Such May Be Found, By Myself, Missus K. E. B. Walker, Colored,* Renaissance Society of the University of Chicago (1997); *Slavery!, Slavery!,* 25th International Biennale of São Paolo (2002); *Narratives of a Negress,* Tang Museum and Williams College (2003); *Kara Walker at the Met: After the Deluge,* Metropolitan Museum of Art, New York (2006); *Harper's Pictorial History of the Civil War (Annotated),* Addison Gallery of American Art, Andover, Mass. (2007); and the 52nd Venice Biennale (2007). *My Complement, My Enemy, My Oppressor, My Love,* a midcareer survey of Walker's work, appeared at the ARC/Musée d'Art Moderne de la Ville, Paris, and toured the United States in 2007 and 2008.   [ACS]

CARRIE MAE WEEMS

(b. 1953, American; lives and works in Syracuse, N.Y.)
Artist and photographer Carrie Mae Weems received a BFA from the California Institute of the Arts, an MFA from the University of California, San Diego, and studied folklore at the University of California, Berkeley. She has created a remarkable body of work that employs photography, sound, text, installation, and video to examine the complexities of family relationships, gender roles, history, racism, sexism, class, and political systems.

The artist often inserts herself within her work as a muse protagonist to bear witness to, explore, and challenge perceptions of race, class, gender, and power. Several of her photographic series—*The Kitchen Table Series* (1990), *From Here I Saw What Happened and I Cried* (1995–96), *The Hampton Album of 1900: The Hampton Project* (2000), and *The Louisiana Project* (2003)—have brought her international acclaim. She began incorporating the moving image into her work in 2003, and has created several video works: *Coming Up for Air* (2003), *Meaning and Landscape* (2004), *A Woman's Journey* (2004), *In Love, In Trouble and Out of Time* (2004), and *Italian Dreams* (2006). In 2005, Weems was the recipient of the Joseph H. Hazen Rome Prize Fellowship from the American Academy in Rome. She has received several other commendations, including the Louis Comfort Tiffany Award (1992), New England Foundation for the Arts, Visual Arts Award (1993), Visual Arts Fellowship, National Endowment for the Arts (1994), Photographer of the Year, Friends of Photography, San Francisco (1994), CalArts / Alpert Award in the Arts (1996), and the Pollock-Krasner Foundation Grant in Photography (2002–3).

Weems's work was the subject of a ten-year survey and a national tour organized by the National Museum of Women in the Arts, Washington, D.C., in 1993. She has been featured in countless national and international exhibitions: *Black Male, Representations of Masculinity in Contemporary American Art* (1994); *Bearing Witness: Contemporary Works by African American Women Artists* (1996); Dak'Art, Dakar Biennale of Contemporary Art, Senegal (1996); *Alternating Currents,* 2nd Johannesburg Biennale (1997); and *Only Skin Deep: Changing Visions of the American Self* (2003). Consistently creating a diverse body of work over the last several decades, she remains one of the most prolific American photographers.   [ACS]

YVONNE WELBON

(b. 1962, American; lives and works in Chicago)
Yvonne Welbon is an independent filmmaker, freelance producer, and writer. Dedicated to presenting the perspectives of traditionally undocumented groups in her critical writing and filmmaking, she uses her position as cultural producer to usurp the traditionalist view of black women's roles in media outlets, specifically film and television. As a

filmmaker, she has created autobiographically driven videos that include African American women and, specifically, African American lesbians. In *Monique* (1991), *Sisters in the Life: First Love* (1993), *Missing Relations* (1994), and *Remembering Wei Yi Fang, Remembering Myself . . .* (1995), Welbon draws on personal experiences and familial narratives to create visual texts that explore race, sexuality, migration, and culture. Her earlier films employ experimental filmmaking techniques to assist in their retelling.

Ensuring that stories on black women that promote identification and understanding are available, Welbon's more recent works have been historically based films that utilize archival footage, interviews, and dramatic reenactments. The award-winning *Living with Pride: Ruth Ellis @ 100* (1999) documents the oldest-known living African American lesbian, while *The Taste of Dirt* (2002) records several women's stories of bruised self-images endured in an adolescence spent on numerous playgrounds in the United States. *Sisters in Cinema* (2003), based on research conducted for Welbon's doctoral dissertation on African American women filmmakers, is a traditional documentary that discusses their lives and work, spanning the early twentieth century to the present. Among her freelance production projects are Zeinabu irene Davis's first full-length feature film, *Compensation* (1999), and Cheryl Dunye's HBO film, *Stranger Inside* (2001).

Welbon's academic career mimics her cinematic one in its conflation of academic and hands-on experiences. She received her BA in History from Vassar College; immediately after graduation, she moved to Taipei, Taiwan, where she taught English, founded and published an arts publication, and acknowledged her interest in filmmaking. She received her MFA from the School of the Art Institute of Chicago, and became the first African American woman to graduate from its film and video program. She obtained a PhD from Northwestern University, and is also a graduate of the American Film Institute's Directing Workshop for Women.

Welbon's films have appeared in more than one hundred festivals around the world and received numerous awards. They have been seen on such cable networks as HBO, the Independent Film Channel (IFC) and the Sundance Channel, as well as on PBS.   [MDH]

PAULA WILSON
(b. 1980, American; lives and works in New York)
Paula Wilson is recognized for her multilayered, complex, and socially relevant paintings that use video and sculpture to discuss issues of memory, power, and sensuality. Wilson received a BFA with honors from Washington University, St. Louis, in 1998, and an MFA from Columbia University in 2005. She is a critic in Painting and Printmaking at the Yale University School of Art.

By working in a combination of media, Wilson provides an interesting collision of relations and oppositions. In single works, she combines video, collage, and painting to bridge seemingly dissimilar media as well as facilitate lively dialogues charged with symbolic images that reference the environment, social histories, and the state of the future. The narrative qualities present key elements traditionally missing from political and social debates on race, class, and gender.

Wilson's work has appeared in galleries and museums in New York, Los Angeles, Chicago, Miami, and Philadelphia. It has also been seen internationally—at the Zacheta National Gallery of Art, Warsaw, and Galleria Suzy Shammah, Milan, where she had a solo exhibition. Wilson was the recipient of the Art Production Fund's Giverny Residency, in Giverny, France, and the Milovich Award in Painting, in St. Louis, Missouri. She was an artist in residence at the Vermont Studio Center, in Johnson, and visiting artist lecturer at Westinghouse School, in Chicago.   [MDH]

LAUREN WOODS

(b. 1979, American; lives and works in San Francisco, California)

Lauren Woods is a multimedia artist who uses single-channel projections and large-scale multichannel video installations to engage history and contemporary perceptions of African diasporic motifs. Woods began her studies at St. Louis University (1997–99), and in Madrid (1999–2000), and completed her undergraduate work in radio, television, and film and Spanish at the University of North Texas, Dallas, in 2002. She pursued further studies at the Universidad de Sagrado Corazon, San Juan, Puerto Rico, and received her MFA in film and video from the San Francisco Art Institute in 2006.

Woods has produced a number of provocative works that examine such topics as the subjective role of the documentary, the black female body, psychology, objectified desire, and sociopolitical philosophy. Her use of highly specialized technological programs and filmmaking techniques is manifested in works that seek to translate the artist's personal experiences into accessible multimedia projects that exist across racial, social, and ethnic divides. Interested in viewing cinema through the lens of public art, Woods also produces site-specific works that discuss race and class in the Jim Crow–era South.

Her films and videos have been screened at such notable festivals and exhibition venues as Yerba Buena Center for the Arts, California; Project Row Houses, Houston; Steve Turner Gallery, Los Angeles; Swarm Gallery, Oakland, California; Korea Broadcasting Institute, Seoul; Festival Experimental, San Juan, Puerto Rico; the Athens International Film and Video Festival; and the Black Film Festival, and International Women of Color Film Festival, in San Francisco; among others. Her work, which has been presented at numerous colleges and universities throughout the United States, is in the collection of the National Taiwan University of Arts. Woods has received grants and awards from the College Art Association, Puffin Foundation, and San Francisco Foundation. In 2008, Woods was awarded a prestigious visual arts grant from Creative Capital.   [MDH]

SELECT BIBLIOGRAPHY

GENERAL READING

Anastas, Rhea, and Michael Brenson. *Witness to Her Art: Art Writings by Adrian Piper, Mona Hatoum, Cady Noland, Jenny Holzer, Kara Walker, Daniela Rossell, and Eau de Cologne.* Annandale-on-Hudson, N.Y.: Bard Center for Curatorial Studies, in association with Hatje Cantz Verlag, 2006.

Bobo, Jacqueline. *Black Women Film and Video Artists.* New York and London: Routledge, 1998.

Broude, Norma, and Mary Garrand, eds. *The Power of Feminist Art.* New York: Harry N. Abrams, 1994.

Duplaix, Sophie. *Sons et Lumières: Une Histoire du son dans l'art du XX Siècle.* Exh. cat. Paris: Centre Georges Pompidou, 2004.

English, Darby. *How to See a Work of Art in Total Darkness.* Cambridge: MIT Press, 2007.

Gianelli, Ida. *Video Art: The Castello di Rivoli Collection.* Exh. cat. Milan: Museo d'Arte Contemporanea, Rivoli-Torino, in association with Skira, 2005.

Goode Bryant, Linda, and Marcy S. Philips. *Contextures.* New York: Just Above Midtown, 1978.

Hanley, Joanna. *The First Generation: Women and Video, 1970–1975.* New York: Independent Curators Incorporated, 1993.

hooks, bell. *Art on My Mind: Visual Politics.* New York: The New Press, 1995.

———. *Black Looks: Race and Representation.* Boston: South End Press, 1992.

hooks, bell, and Leslie King-Hammond. *Gumbo Ya-Ya: An Anthology of Contemporary African American Women Artists.* New York: Midmarch Press, 1995.

———. *Outlaw Culture: Resisting Representations.* London: Routledge, 2006.

Lippard, Lucy. *Get the Message! A Decade of Art for Social Change.* New York: E. P. Dutton, 1984.

Lord, Catherine, and Charles Gaines. *The Theatre of Refusal: Black Art and the Mainstream.* Exh. cat. Irvine: University of California Fine Arts Gallery, 1993.

Martin, Sylvia. *Video Art.* Cologne: Taschen, 2006.

Matthews, Nancy Mowll. *Moving Pictures: American Art and Early Film, 1880–1910.* Exh. cat. Manchester, Vt.: Hudson Hills Press, with Williams College Museum of Art, 2005.

Mills, Charles W. *Blackness Visible: Essays on Philosophy and Race.* Ithaca and London: Cornell University Press, 1998.

Molesworth, Helen. *Image Stream.* Exh. cat. Columbus: Wexner Center for the Arts, Ohio State University, 2004.

Morrison, Toni. *Playing in the Dark: Whiteness and the Literary Imagination.* New York: Vintage Books, 1993.

Moten, Fred. *In the Break: The Aesthetics of the Black Radical Tradition.* Minneapolis: University of Minnesota Press, 2003.

Neumaier, Diane, ed. *Reframings: New American Feminist Photographers.* Philadelphia: Temple University Press, 1995.

Rodgers-Rose, La Francis, ed. *The Black Woman.* London: Sage Publications, 1980.

St. Jean, Yanick, and Joe R. Feagin, eds. *Double Burden: Black Women and Everyday Racism.* New York: M. E. Sharpe, 1998.

Shimmel, Paul, ed. *Out of Actions: Between Performance and the Object.* Exh. cat. Los Angeles: Museum of Contemporary Art, in association with Thames and Hudson, London, 1998.

Shohat, Ella, ed. *Talking Visions: Multicultural Feminism in a Transnational Age.* Cambridge: MIT Press; New York: New Museum of Contemporary Art, 1998.

Smith, Valerie. *Not Just Race, Not Just Gender: Black Feminist Readings.* London: Routledge, 1998.

www.sistersincinema.com, accessed November 10, 2007.

Willis, Deborah, and Carla Williams. *The Black Female Body: A Photographic History.* Philadelphia: Temple University Press, 2002.

EXHIBITION CATALOGUES AND BOOKS FEATURING ARTISTS IN CINEMA REMIXED & RELOADED

Alvim, Fernando. *Observatorio/Observatory*. Exh. cat. Valencía: Institute of Modern Art, 2006.

Baume, Nicholas, Wayne Koestenbaum, and Jennifer Doyle, eds. *Getting Emotional*. Exh. cat. Boston: Institute of Contemporary Art, 2005.

Bontemps, Jacqueline Fonvielle, and Arna Alexander Bontemps. *Forever Free: Art by African American Women, 1862–1980*. Exh. cat. Normal: Jocelyn Art Museum, Illinois State University, 1981.

Brewinska, Maria, ed. *Black Alphabet: Contexts of Contemporary African American Art*. Exh. cat. Warsaw: Zacheta National Gallery of Art, 2006.

Butler, Connie, ed. *WACK! Art and the Feminist Revolution*. Exh. cat. Los Angeles: Museum of Contemporary Art, in association with MIT Press, Cambridge, 2007.

Cassel Oliver, Valerie, ed. *Black Light/White Noise: Sound and Light in Contemporary Art*. Exh. cat. Houston: Contemporary Arts Museum, 2007.

———, ed. *Double Consciousness: Black Conceptual Art Since 1970*. Exh. cat. Houston: Contemporary Arts Museum, 2005.

Corris, Michael, ed. *Conceptual Art: Theory, Myth, and Practice*. New York: Cambridge University Press, 2004.

Czekelius, Annette, and Michael Thoss, eds. *Portrat Afrika*. Exh. cat. Munich: House of World Cultures, 2000.

Dadi, Iftikhar, and Salah Hassan. *Unpacking Europe*. Exh. cat. Rotterdam: Museum Boijmans Van Beuningen, in association with NAi Publishers, 2002.

Dent, Gina, ed. *Black Popular Culture (A Project by Michele Wallace)*. Seattle: Bay Press, 1992.

Enwesor, Okwui, ed. *Trade Routes: History and Geography*. Exh. cat. Johannesburg: Africus Institute for Contemporary Art, 1997.

———, et al. *Documenta XI*. Exh. cat. Ostfildern-Ruit, Germany: Hatje Cantz Verlag, 2002.

Fusco, Coco, and Brian Wallis, eds. *Only Skin Deep: Changing Visions of the American Self*. Exh. cat. New York: International Center of Photography, in association with Harry N. Abrams, 2004.

Gangitano, Lia, and Steven Nelson, eds. *New Histories*. Exh. cat. Boston: Institute of Contemporary Art, 1996.

George, Adrian, ed. *art, lies and videotape: exposing performance*. Exh. cat. London: Tate Liverpool, 2003.

Glenn, Constance, ed. *Reconfiguring Boundaries/Defining Spaces: Maren Hassinger, Frederick Fisher, Eugenia Butler*. Exh. cat. Long Beach: University Art Museum, California State University, 1994.

Goldberg, Roselee. *Performance: Live Art Since the 60s*. London: Thames and Hudson, 1998.

Golden, Thelma. *Black Male: Representations of Masculinity in Contemporary American Art*. Exh. cat. New York: Whitney Museum of American Art, in association with Harry N. Abrams, 1994.

———, and Christine Kim, eds. *Frequency*. Exh. cat. New York: Studio Museum in Harlem, 2005.

Gollinski, Hans Günter, and Shepp Hiekisch-Picard, eds. Exh. cat. *New Identities: Zeitgenössische Kunst aus Südafrika*. Bochum, Germany: Museum Bochum, in association with Hatje Cantz Verlag, 2005.

Harney, Elizabeth. *TEXTures: Word and Symbol in Contemporary African Art*. Exh. cat. (website: www.nmafa.si.edu/exhibits/textures). Washington, D.C.: Smithsonian National Museum of African Art, 2005.

Hassan, Salah, and Olu Oguibe, eds. *Authentic/Excentric: Conceptualism in Contemporary African Art*. Exh. cat. Ithaca, N.Y.: Forum for African Arts, Inc., 2001.

Heartney, Eleanor. *After the Revolution: Women Who Transformed Contemporary Art*. Columbus, Ohio: Merrell Publishers, 2007.

Herbert, Lynn, and Paola Morsiani. *Out of the Ordinary: New Art from Texas*. Exh. cat. Houston: Contemporary Arts Museum, 2000.

Iles, Chrissie, and Philippe Vergne. *Whitney Biennial 2006: Day for Night*. Exh. cat. New York: Whitney Museum of American Art, 2006.

Ilesanmi, Olukemi. *The Squared Circle: Boxing in Contemporary Art*. Exh. cat. Minneapolis: Walker Art Center, 2003.

Jones, Kellie. *Life's Little Necessities: Installations by Women in the 1990s*. Johannesburg: 2nd Johannesburg Biennale, 1997.

King-Hammond, Leslie, and Lowery Stokes Sims. *Art as a Verb—The Evolving Continuum: Installations, Performances, and Videos by 13 Afro-American Artists*. Exh. cat. Baltimore: Maryland Institute College of Art, 1988.

Koehler, Eric, ed. *DAK'ART 2000*. Exh. cat. Senegal: La Biennale de l'Art African Contemporain, 2000.

Konatè, Yacouba, ed. *DAK'ART 2006*. Exh. cat. Senegal: La Biennale de l'Art African Contemporain, 2006.

Kress, Laus, John Ashbery, Gerald M. Edelman, et al. *Whitney Biennial 1995*. Exh. cat. New York: Whitney Museum of American Art, in association with Harry N. Abrams, 1995.

Kuramitsu, Kris, and Lizzetta LeFalle-Collins. *Linkages & Themes in the African Diaspora: Selections from the Eileen Harris Norton and Peter Norton Art Collections*. Exh. cat. San Francisco: Museum of the African Diaspora, 2005.

Langford, Martha, and Peter Feldstein. *Image and Imagination*. Exh. cat. Montreal: McGill-Queen's University Press, 2005.

LeFalle-Collins, Lizzetta. *Dispersed: African Legacy/New World Reality*. Exh. cat. San Francisco: Museum of the African Diaspora, 2006.

Martin, Jean-Hubert. *Africa Remix*. Exh. cat. Munich: Hatje Cantz Verlag, 2005.

Martin, Marilyn, Simon Njami, et al. *Coexistence: Contemporary Cultural Production in South Africa*. Exh. cat. Cape Town: South African National Gallery; Waltham, Mass: Rose Art Museum, Brandeis University, 2004.

Mills, Kathleen, Robin Brentano, and Olivia Georgia. *Outside the Frame: Performance and the Object*. Exh. cat. Cleveland: Center for Contemporary Art, 1994.

Muhammad, Erika. *Race into Digital Space*. Exh. cat. Cambridge: List Visual Arts Center, MIT, 2001.

Peraza, Nilda, Marcia Tucker, Kinshasha Conwill, Eunice Lipton, et al. *The Decade Show: Frameworks of Identity in the 1980s*. Exh. cat. New York: New Museum of Contemporary Art, Studio Museum in Harlem, and Museum of Contemporary Hispanic Art, 1990.

Phillips, Lisa. *The American Century: Art and Culture, 1950–2000*. Exh. cat. New York: Whitney Museum of American Art, 1999.

———, and Louise Neri. *Whitney Biennial 1997*. Exh. cat. New York: Whitney Museum of American Art, in association with Harry N. Abrams, 1997.

Powell, Richard J. *Black Art and Culture in the 20th Century*. London: Thames and Hudson, 1997.

Pustola, Magda, and Aneta Szylak. *You Won't Feel a Thing: On Panic, Obsession, Rituality and Anesthesia*. Exh. cat. Gdansk: WYSPA Institute of Art, in collaboration with Kunsthaus Dresden, 2007.

Read, Alan, ed. *The Fact of Blackness: Frantz Fanon and Visual Representation*. London: Institute of Contemporary Art and Institute of International Visual Arts, in association with Bay Press, Seattle, 1996.

Reenberg, Holger. *Socle du Monde*. Exh. cat. Herning, Denmark: Herning Kunstmuseum, 2006.

Reilly, Maura, and Linda Nochlin, eds. *Global Feminisms: New Directions in Contemporary Art*. Exh. cat. New York: Brooklyn Museum, in association with Prestel Publishers, Munich, 2007.

Rinder, Lawrence. *Whitney Biennial 2002*. Exh. cat. New York: Whitney Museum of American Art, 2002.

Robinson, Jontyle, Beverly Guy-Sheftan, Lowery Stokes Sims, Judith Wilson, et al. *Bearing Witness: Contemporary Works by African American Women Artists*. Exh. cat. Atlanta: Spelman College Museum of Fine Art, in association with Rizzoli International Publications, 1996.

Schoonmaker, Trevor. *Black President: The Art and Legacy of Fela Anikulapo-Kuti*. Exh. cat. New York: The New Museum, 2003.

Scott, Deirdre, Kinshasha Conwill, Lowery Stokes Sims, and Frank Steward. *Passage: Contemporary Art in Transition*. Exh. cat. New York: Studio Museum in Harlem, 1999.

Sobel, Dean. *Identity Crisis: Self-Portraiture at the End of the Century*. Exh. cat. Milwaukee: Milwaukee Art Museum, 1997.

Storr, Robert. *Disparities and Deformations: Our Grotesque*. Exh. cat. Santa Fe, N.M.: Site Santa Fe, 2004.

Sussman, Elizabeth. *Whitney Biennial 1993*. Exh. cat. New York: Whitney Museum of American Art, 1993.

Wallace, Michele, ed. *Black Macho and the Myth of the Superwoman*. New York: Dial Press, 1970.

Wendt, Selene. *Equatorial Rhythms*. Exh. cat. Oslo: Sternersen Museum, 2007.

Wiehager, Renate, ed. *Moving Pictures: Photography and Film in Contemporary Art*. Exh. cat. New York: Solomon R. Guggenheim Museum, in association with Hatje Cantz Verlag, 2001.

Wilson, Judith, Steven Nelson, Jean Fisher, and Rena Wolf. *New Histories*. Exh. cat. Boston: Institute of Contemporary Art, 1997.

MONOGRAPHS AND ONE-PERSON-EXHIBITION CATALOGUES

MARÍA MAGDALENA CAMPOS-PONS

Beauchamp-Byrd, Mora. *María Magdelena Campos-Pons: When I Am Not Here/Estoy Alla*. Exh. cat. New York: Franklin H. Williams Caribbean Cultural Center/African Diaspora Institute, 1997.

Freiman, Lisa, and Okwui Enwesor. *María Magdalena Campos-Pons: Everything Is Separated by Water*. Exh. cat. Indianapolis: Indianapolis Museum of Art, in association with Yale University Press, 2007.

Riddell, Jennifer, and Michael D. Harris. *María Magdelena Campos-Pons: Meanwhile, the Girls Were Playing*. Exh. cat. Cambridge: List Visual Arts Center, MIT, 1999.

Spoken Softly with Mama. Exh. cat. New York: Museum of Modern Art; Ottawa: National Gallery of Canada, 1998.

Wendt, Selene. *One Thousand Ways to Say Goodbye*. Exh. cat. Oslo: Henie Onstad Kunstsenter, 2003.

STEPHANIE DINKINS

Dinkins, Stephanie. *Stephanie Dinkins: Photography Retrospective, 1956–1986*. Exh. cat. New Orleans: Simms Fine Art Gallery, 1987.

LEAH GILLIAM

Gilliam, Leah. *Project Rooms*. Exh. cat. New York: Thread Waxing Space, 1999.

———, and Lia Gangitano. *Apeshit v.3*. Exh. cat. New York: Thread Waxing Space, 1999.

RENÉE GREEN

Ferguson, Russell, ed. *World Tour/Renée Green*. Exh. cat. Los Angeles: Museum of Contemporary Art, 1993.

Green, Renée. *Renée Green: Between and Including*. Exh. cat. Vienna: Vienna Secession, 2001.

———. *Sombras y señales = Shadows and Signals*. Exh. cat. Barcelona: Fundació Antoni Tapies, 2000.

Van Duyn, Edna, Angela Cumberbrich, and Jodokuns Driessen. *Renée Green*. Exh. cat. Amsterdam: De Appel Foundation, 1996.

MAREN HASSINGER

Collischan van Wagner, Judy. *Maren Hassinger 1972–1991*. Exh. cat. Brookville, N.Y.: Hillwood Art Museum, Long Island University, 1991.

Hart, Katherine. *Maren Hassinger: On Dangerous Ground*. Exh. cat. Los Angeles: Los Angeles County Museum of Art, 1981.

BRADLEY MCCALLUM AND JACQUELINE TARRY

McCallum, Bradley, Jacqueline Tarry, and David Spalding. *Whitewash*. Monograph. Hong Kong: Timezone 8, 2007.

Sirmans, Franklin. *McCallum and Tarry: Civil Endurance*. Exh. cat. Washington, D.C.: Conner Contemporary, 2003.

TRACEY MOFFATT

Berg, Stefan, Brigette Reinhardt, and Alexander Tolnay. eds. *Tracey Moffatt: Laudanum*. Ostfildern-Ruit, Germany: Hatje Cantz Verlag, 1999.

Cooke, Lynn, and Isaac Julien. *Tracey Moffatt: Free-Falling*. Exh. cat. New York: Dia Art Foundation, 1998.

Durand, Regis. *Tracey Moffatt*. Madrid: Fundacion la Caixa de Pensìones, 1999.

Newton, Gael, and Tracey Moffatt. *Tracey Moffatt: Fever Pitch*. Sydney: Piper Press, 1995.

Snelling, Michael. ed. *Tracey Moffatt*. Exh. cat. Brisbane: Institute of Modern Art, Australia, 2001.

Summerhayes, Catherine. *The Moving Images of Tracey Moffatt*. Milan: Charta Publishers, 2007.

WANGECHI MUTU

Boswell, Peter. *Wangechi Mutu—Amazing Grace*. Exh. cat. Miami: Miami Art Museum, 2005.

McDowell, Tara. *New Work: Wangechi Mutu*. Exh. cat. San Francisco: San Francisco Museum of Modern Art, 2005.

HOWARDENA PINDELL

Elsas, Ellen F., and Howardena Pindell. *Howardena Pindell: Traveler's Memories, Japan Series*. Exh. cat. Birmingham, Ala.: Birmingham Museum of Art, 1984.

Pindell, Howardena. *The Heart of the Matter: The Writings and Paintings of Howardena Pindell*. Exh. cat. New York: Midmarch Arts Press, 1997.

———. *Howardena Pindell: Autobiography*. Exh. cat. New York: Cyrus Gallery, 1989.

———. *Howardena Pindell: Odyssey*. Exh. cat. New York: Studio Museum in Harlem, 1986.

Stanislaus, Grace, Holland Cotter, and Lowery Stokes Sims. *Howardena Pindell: Paintings and Drawings, A Retrospective Exhibition, 1972–1992*. Exh. cat. Kansas City, Mo.: Exhibits U.S.A.; Potsdam, N.Y.: Gibson Gallery, State University of New York, 1992.

ADRIAN PIPER

Berger, Maurice, and Jean Fisher. *Adrian Piper: A Retrospective 1965–2000*. Exh. cat. Baltimore: University of Maryland Fine Arts Gallery, 1999.

Faver, Jane. *Adrian Piper: Reflections 1967–1987*. Exh. cat. New York: Alternative Museum, 1987.

Piper, Adrian. *Adrian Piper*. Exh. cat. Birmingham, England: Ikon Gallery, 1991.

———. *Out of Order, Out of Sight: Selected Writings in Meta-Art, 1968–1992*. 2 vols. Cambridge: MIT Press, 1996.

———. *Texts d'oeuvres et essays*. Exh. cat. Villeurbanne, France: Institut d'art contemporain, 2003.

———, and Sabine Breitwieser. *Metakunst und Kunstkrik*. Exh. cat. Vienna: Generali Foundation, 2002.

BERNI SEARLE

Baderoon, Gabeba, Laurie Ann Farrell, and Clive Kellner. *Berni Searle: Approach*. Exh. cat. Cape Town: Michael Stevenson Gallery, in association with Contemporary Art Museum/Institute for Research in Art, University of South Florida, Tampa, and Johannesburg Art Gallery, 2006.

Bester, Rory. *Berni Searle: Float*. Monograph. Cape Town: Michael Stevenson Gallery, 2003.

Coombes, Annie. *Berni Searle: Fresh*. Exh. cat. Cape Town: South African National Gallery of Art, 2003.

Hassan, Salah. *Berni Searle: Self and Other*. Exh. bro. New York: Apex Art, 2000.

Jacobson, Heidi Zuckerman. *Berni Searle/Matrix 202: A Matter of Time*. Exh. bro. Berkeley, Calif.: Berkeley Art Museum and Pacific Film Archive, 2003.

Searle, Berni. *Berni Searle: About to Forget*. Monograph. Cape Town: Michael Stevenson Gallery, 2005.

Stevenson, Michael. *Berni Searle: Vapour*. Monograph. Cape Town: Michael Stevenson Gallery, 2004.

———, and Katherine Smith. *Berni Searle: Darker Shades of Light*. Exh. cat. Sandton, South Africa: FNB Vita Art Prize 2000, in association with Sandton Civic Gallery, 2000.

XAVIERA SIMMONS

Cassel Oliver, Valerie, and Xaviera Simmons. *Perspectives 157: Xaviera Simmons*. Houston: Contemporary Arts Museum, 2007.

LORNA SIMPSON

Enwesor, Okwui, Helaine Posner, Hilton Als, and Issac Julien. *Scenarios: Recent Work by Lorna Simpson*. Exh. cat. New York: American Federation for the Arts, in association with Harry N. Abrams, 2007.

Jones, Kellie, Thelma Golden, and Chrissie Iles. *Lorna Simpson*. Monograph. London: Phaidon Press, 2002.

Simpson, Lorna, and Sarah J. Rogers. *Lorna Simpson: Interior/Exterior, Full/Empty*. Exh. cat. Columbus: Wexner Center for the Arts, Ohio State University, 1997.

Willis, Deborah. *Lorna Simpson: Untitled 54*. Monograph. San Francisco: The Friends of Photography, 1992.

Wright, Beryl, and Saidiya V. Hartman. *Lorna Simpson: For the Sake of the Viewer*. Exh. cat. Chicago: Museum of Contemporary Art, in association with Universe Publishers, 1992.

CAULEEN SMITH

Smith, Cauleen, and Van Jordan. *I Want to See My Skirt*. Exh. cat. Austin, Tex.: Fluent-Collaborative test site, 2006.

KARA WALKER

Berry, Ian, Darby English, and Vivian Patterson, eds. *Narratives of a Negress*. Skidmore, N.Y.: Tang Museum and Williams College, in association with MIT Press, 2003.

Dixon, Annette. *Kara Walker: Pictures from Another Time*. Exh. cat. Ann Arbor: University of Michigan Museum of Fine Art, 2002.

DuBois Shaw, Gwendolyn. *Seeing the Unspeakable: The Art of Kara Walker*. Durham, N.C.: Duke University Press, 2004.

Vergne, Philippe, Sander Gilman, Thomas McEvilley, et al. *My Complement, My Enemy, My Oppressor, My Love*. Exh. cat. Minneapolis: Walker Art Center, 2007.

Walker, Kara. *Kara Walker: After the Deluge*. Exh. cat. New York: Metropolitan Museum of Art, in association with Rizzoli International Publications, 2007.

——. *Presenting Negro Scenes Drawn Upon My Passage Through the South and Reconfigured for the Benefit of Enlightened Audiences Wherever Such May Be Found, By Myself, Missus K. E. B. Walker, Colored*. Exh. cat. Chicago: Renaissance Society of the University of Chicago, 1997.

CARRIE MAE WEEMS

Baker, Houston, and bell hooks. *Carrie Mae Weems: In These Islands*. Birmingham: University of Alabama Press, 1995.

Cahan, Susan, and Pamela R. Metzer. *Carrie Mae Weems: The Louisiana Project*. Exh. cat. New Orleans: Newcomb Art Gallery, in association with University of Washington Press, 2005.

Hirsh, Andrea, and Susan Fisher Stirling. *Carrie Mae Weems*. Exh. cat. Washington, D.C.: National Museum of Women in the Arts, in association with Northeastern University Press, 1993.

Patterson, Vivian, and Frederick Randolph. *Carrie Mae Weems: The Hampton Project*. Williamstown, Mass.: Williams College Museum of Art, in association with Aperture, 2001.

Pinche, Jr., Thomas, and Thelma Golden. *Carrie Mae Weems: Recent Work 1992–1998*. Exh. cat. New York: George Braziller, 2003.

SELECT FILMOGRAPHY

CAMILLE BILLOPS

Suzanne, Suzanne. 16mm, b/w, 26 minutes, 1982.
Older Women in Love. 16mm, color, 26 minutes, 1987.
Finding Christa. 16mm, color, 60 minutes, 1991.
The KKK Boutique Ain't Just for Rednecks. 16mm, color, 77 minutes, 1994.
Take Your Bags. 16mm, color, 11 minutes, 1998–99.
A String of Pearls. 16mm, color, 57 minutes, 2002.

CARROLL PARROTT BLUE

Two Women. 16mm, color, 10 minutes, 1977–79.
Vanette's World: A Study of a Young Artist. 16mm, color, 26 minutes, 1979.
Conversations with Roy DeCarava. 16mm, color, 28 minutes, 1983.
Smithsonian World: Nigerian Art: Kindred Spirits. Video, color, 60 minutes, 1990.
Mystery of the Senses: Vision. 16mm, color, 60 minutes, 1993–94.
The Dawn at My Back. Interactive media, 2005.
Dubai. Video, color, 5 minutes, 2005.
Thelma Scott Bryant and Third Ward: An Urban Redevelopment Story. Video, color, 5 minutes, 2006.
The Third Ward Story Mapping Project. Interactive media, 2006.

AYOKA CHENZIRA

Syvilla: They Dance to Her Drum. 16mm, color, 25 minutes, 1979.
Hairpiece: A Film for Nappyheaded People. 16mm, animated, color, 10 minutes, 1984.
The Lure and the Lore. Video, color, 15 minutes, 1988.
Zajota and the Boogie Spirit. 16mm, animated, color, 20 minutes, 1989.
Pull Your Head to the Moon: Creole Stories. 16mm, color, 12 minutes, 1992.
Alma's Rainbow. 35mm, color, 85 minutes, 1993.
My Own TV (MOTV). 16mm, color, 54 minutes, 1993.
Sentry at the Gate. Video, color, 56 minutes, 1995.

JULIE DASH

Four Women. 16mm, color, 4 minutes, 1975.
Diary of an African Nun. 16mm, b/w, 13:30 minutes, 1977.
Illusions. 16mm, b/w, 34 minutes, 1983.
Daughters of the Dust. 35mm, color, 114 minutes, 1991.
Praise House. Video, color, 27 minutes, 1991.

ZEINABU irene DAVIS

Filmstatement. 16mm, b/w, 13 minutes, 1982.
Re-creating Black Women's Media Image. Video, color, 30 minutes, 1983.
Crocodile Conspiracy. 16mm, color, 13 minutes, 1986.
Sweet Bird of Youth. Video, color, 5 minutes, 1987.
Cycles. 16mm, b/w, 17 minutes, 1989.
Trumpetistically, Cora Bryant. Video, color, 5 minutes, 1989.
A Period Piece. Video, color, 4 minutes, 1991.
A Powerful Thang. 16mm, color, 57 minutes, 1991.
Mother of the River. 16mm, b/w, 30 minutes, 1995.
Compensation. Video, b/w, 92 minutes, 1999.
Trumpetistically, Cora Bryant. 16mm and digital video, color, 55 minutes, 2004.

CHERYL DUNYE

Janine. Video, color, 9 minutes, 1990.
She Don't Fade. Video, b/w, 23 minutes, 1991.
Vanilla Sex. Video, b/w, 5 minutes, 1992.
The Potluck and the Passion. Video, color, 22 minutes, 1992.
Complicated Flesh, with Kristina Deutsch. Video, color, 14 minutes, 1993.
Untitled Portrait. Video, b/w, 5 minutes, 1993.
Greetings from Africa. 16mm, color and b/w, 10 minutes, 1994.
Watermelon Woman. 16mm feature-length film, color and b/w, 85 minutes, 1996.
The Stranger Inside. 16mm feature-length film, color, 90 minutes, 2000.
My Baby's Daddy. 16mm feature-length film, color, 86 minutes, 2003.

SHARI FRILOT

Flyboy. Video, color, 7 minutes, 1989.
A Cosmic Demonstration of Sexuality. Video, color, 15 minutes, 1993.
What Is a Line? Video, color, 10 minutes, 1994.
Black Nations/Queer Nations. Video, color, 50 minutes, 1995.
Strange and Charmed. Video, color, 16 minutes, 2003.

LEAH GILLIAM

Now Pretend. 16mm, b/w, 10 minutes, 1991.
Sapphire and the Slave Girl. Video, b/w, 17:30 minutes, 1995.
Apeshit. 8mm, color and b/w, 6 minutes, 1999.
Apeshit v.3. Interactive media, 1999.
Agenda for a Landscape. Interactive media, 2001.
Playing the Race Card. Video, color, 8 minutes, 2001.

PAMELA L. JENNINGS

The Silence That Allows. Video, color, 38 minutes, 1990.

I've Never. Video, b/w, 5 minutes, 1992.

Sleep Now Variations. Video, color, 5 minutes, 1992.

My House. Interactive media, 1993.

Night Trees. Interactive media, 1993.

The Balance. Interactive media, 1993.

Solitaire. Interactive media, 1994.

BARBARA MCCULLOUGH

Water Ritual #1: An Urban Rite of Purification. 16mm, b/w, 4 minutes, 1979.

Fragments. 16mm, color, 10 minutes, 1980.

The World Saxophone Quartet. 16mm, color, 5 minutes, 1980.

Shopping Bag Spirits and Freeway Fetishes: Reflections on Ritual Space. Video, color, 60 minutes, 1981.

YVETTE MATTERN

Strings. Video, color, 10 minutes, 1992.

Sublime Viscera. Video, color, 12 minutes, 1992.

Pearl. 16mm, Super 8mm, video, color and b/w, 94 minutes, 1994.

Wax Tails. Video, b/w, 6 minutes, 1996.

The Zanzibar Project. Video, color, 12 minutes, 1998.

Flash Africa. Video, color, 3 minutes, 2000.

Hijack. Video, color, 18 minutes, 2002.

Heroes, with Robin Arthur. Video, color, 21 minutes, 2004.

Analog. Video, color, 56 minutes, 2006.

MICHELLE DENISE PARKERSON

Sojourn. 16mm, color and b/w , 10 minutes, 1973.

But Then, She's Betty Carter. 16mm, color, 53 minutes, 1980.

Gotta Make This Journey: Sweet Honey in the Rock. Video, color, 58 minutes, 1983.

Stormé: The Lady of the Jewel Box. 16mm, color, 21 minutes, 1987.

Odds and Ends. Video, color, 30 minutes, 1993.

A Litany for Survival: The Life and Work of Audre Lorde, with Ada Gay Griffin. 16mm, color, 88 minutes, 1995.

EVE SANDLER

The Wash: A Cleaning Story. Video, color, 9 minutes, 1999.

CAULEEN SMITH

Daily Rains. 16mm, color, 12 minutes, 1991.

Chronicles of a Lying Spirit by Kelly Gabron. 16mm, color, 6 minutes, 1992.

Sapphire Tapes: Message #1. 16mm, color, 8 minutes, 1993.

A Thousand Words. 16mm, color, 14 minutes, 1995.

White Suit. 16mm, color, 5 minutes, 1997.

Drylongso. 16mm, color, 87 minutes, 1998.

The Changing Same. Digital video, color, sound, 5:30 minutes, 1998–2001.

The Green Dress. 35mm, color, 16 minutes, 2005.

JOCELYN TAYLOR

Be a Diva, with DIVA-TV. Video, color, 58 minutes, 1990.

Father Knows Best. Video, color, 20 minutes, 1990.

I Object (with the House of Color). Video, color, 5 minutes, 1990.

Looking for LaBelle. Video, color and b/w, 5 minutes, 1991.

24 Hours a Day. Video, color, 9 minutes, 1993.

Frankie and Jocie. Video, color, 18 minutes, 1994.

Bodily Functions. Video, color and b/w, 20 minutes, 1995.

I Am the Kingdom. 16mm, color, 30 minutes, 2007.

YVONNE WELBON

Monique. 16mm, color, 3 minutes, 1991.

Cinematic Jazz of Julie Dash. Video, color, 26 minutes, 1993

Sisters in the Life: First Love. Video, color, 23 minutes, 1993.

Missing Relations. Video, color, 13 minutes, 1994.

Remembering Wei Yi Fang, Remembering Myself. Video, color and b/w, 30 minutes, 1995.

Living with Pride: Ruth Ellis @ 100. Video, color, 60 minutes, 1999.

The Taste of Dirt. 16mm, color, 12 minutes, 2003.

CONTRIBUTORS

ABOUT THE CURATORS

Andrea Barnwell Brownlee, PhD, is an art historian, curator, writer, critic, and the director of the Spelman College Museum of Fine Art. Her primary research interests are African American and black British art. She has organized exhibitions, including *iona rozeal brown: a³ . . . black on both sides* (2004) and *Amalia Amaki: Boxes, Buttons and the Blues* (2005). She also cocurated several exhibitions: *Engaging the Camera: African Women, Portraits and the Photographs of Hector Acebes* (2004) and *Hale Woodruff, Nancy Elizabeth Prophet and the Academy* (2007). In addition to the catalogues that accompanied the exhibitions, she has written for such major publications as *To Conserve a Legacy: American Art from Historically Black Colleges and Universities, Rhapsodies in Black: The Art of the Harlem Renaissance,* and *African Americans in Art: Selections from the Art Institute of Chicago.* In 1999, she organized and was principal author of the catalogue for *The Walter O. Evans Collection of African American Art.*

Brownlee is the recipient of numerous academic, professional, and scholarly awards, including a MacArthur Curatorial Fellowship in the department of modern and contemporary art at the Art Institute of Chicago (1998–2000), a Future Women Leadership Award from ArtTable (2005), and the President's Award from the Women's Caucus for Art (2005). An alumna of Spelman College, she completed her master's and doctorate degrees in art history at Duke University. Her monograph *Charles White: The David C. Driskell Series of African American Art, Volume I,* was published by Pomegranate Communications in 2002. Brownlee currently serves on the boards of the Hambidge Center for the Creative Arts and Sciences and the Metropolitan Atlanta Arts Fund. In 2007, she was a juror for the Museum of Contemporary Art Georgia Working Artists Project and vice chair of the City of Atlanta Arts Funding Task Force.

Valerie Cassel Oliver is curator at the Contemporary Arts Museum Houston. Before that, she was director of the Visiting Artists Program at the School of the Art Institute of Chicago (1996–2000) and program specialist at the National Endowment for the Arts (1988–95). In 2000, she served as cocurator of the biennial exhibition at the Whitney Museum of American Art, in New York.

In her position at the Contemporary Arts Museum Houston, Cassel Oliver has organized numerous exhibitions, including *Splat Boom Pow! The Influence of Cartoons in Contemporary Art* (2003) and *Double Consciousness: Black Conceptual Art Since 1970* (2005). She has organized several solo exhibitions, including the first American museum exhibitions for Ghada Amer, Demetrius Oliver, Robert Pruitt, and Xaviera Simmons. She recently opened the group exhibition *Black Light/White Noise: Light and Sound in Contemporary Art* (2007), and is currently planning a retrospective on the work of Fluxus artist Benjamin Patterson (2009).

Cassel Oliver serves on the board of directors for the Aurora Picture Show, a microcinema in Houston, and ArtTable, a national organization for women professionals in the visual arts. She also serves in an advisory capacity for the journals *Callaloo* and *ART LIES,* as well as on the advisory and steering committees for MoAD (Museum of the African Diaspora), San Francisco; Independent Curators International, New York; RxArt, New York; and Etant Donnes, New York/Paris.

Cassel Oliver is a graduate of the University of Texas, Austin, and holds an MA in art history from Howard University.

ABOUT THE CONTRIBUTORS

Isolde Brielmaier, PhD, is an independent project consultant, curator, writer, visiting assistant professor of art at Vassar College, and guest professor at Columbia University/Barnard College. She has developed programs and special events for several clients, including ARCO Contemporary Art Fair, Madrid; Art Chicago; and Candela Music and Art Festival, San Juan, Puerto Rico, as well as venues in New York, Los Angeles, Cleveland, and Atlanta. As curator, she has supported contemporary artists and generated important discussion about their work through her exhibitions in the United States and abroad—most recently, *Maximum Flavor,* Atlanta College of Art Gallery (2005); *Andrew Dosunmu: The African Game* (with Knox Robinson), Reed Space, New York (2006); *CityScapes NYC,* ARCO Contemporary Art Fair, Madrid (2006); *Lee Quinones: PRELUDE,* Galería Candela, Old San Juan, Puerto Rico (2006); and *Pais de Poetas* (with Omar Lopez-Chahoud), Rotunda Gallery, New York (2007). Brielmaier has lectured and published widely: Parkett Series with Contemporary Artists; Aperture; Phaidon Press; Museum of Contemporary Art, Los Angeles; Solomon R. Guggenheim Museum, New York; Brooklyn Museum, New York; Studio Museum in Harlem, New York; Atlanta College of Art Gallery; Harvard University; and Howard University. She holds a PhD from Columbia University, and is based in New York.

Rhea L. Combs, a curator, writer, and doctoral candidate in American studies and film history at Emory University's Graduate Institute of the Liberal Arts, is currently completing her dissertation, entitled "Exceeding the Frame: Documentary Filmmaker Marlon T. Riggs as Cultural Agitator." From 2004 to 2006, she was director of outreach at the National Black Programming Consortium, New York, where she curated the Prized Pieces Film Festival, an annual international film competition that showcases films and programs about human rights and social justice from a uniquely black perspective. Her other curatorial projects include *Voices: Young Directors Under 30* at the Institute of Contemporary Arts, London, and *100 Years of Black Film* at the Smithsonian Institution's National Museum of American History. Combs's writing has been featured in the *Journal of American Folklife* and in the book *What Your Mama Never Told You: True Stories About Sex and Love.* During her tenure, from 2002 to 2004, as curatorial assistant at the Spelman College Museum of Fine Art, she assisted with the exhibitions *iona rozeal brown: a³. . . black on both sides, Amalia Amaki: Boxes, Buttons and the Blues,* and *Hale Woodruff, Nancy Elizabeth Prophet and the Academy.* Combs completed her master's degree at Cornell University in African American studies and her BA at Howard University in radio-television-film. She has taught courses in "Visual Culture," "African American Cinema," and "Race, Gender, and Popular Culture," at Emory University, Chicago State University, and Cornell University, respectively; she also has been a guest lecturer and presented talks on queer film, black feminism, cultural pluralism, and museum studies. Combs is the recipient of several honors, including a prestigious American Association of University Women American Dissertation Completion Fellowship (2007) and the Rockefeller-Emory University Fellowship in Cultural History (2002). She has served as panelist for the New York State Council for the Arts Electronic Media Department (2004–7), and is currently on the board of the Global Action project, an international youth media-arts organization committed to teaching young people how to use media as a tool for social justice.

Romi Crawford is curator and director of education and public programs at the Studio Museum in Harlem and assistant professor of liberal arts and visual critical studies at the School of the Art Institute of Chicago. From 2001 to 2006, she was director of the latter's Visiting

Artists Program, producing arts-related lecture series and symposia. Crawford founded the Crawford and Sloan Gallery, where she curated such exhibitions as *Group Retrospective: Selected African-American Photographers 1973–1993* (1993), and *Urban Style Politics* (1991). More recent curatorial projects include *Contemporary Art and Celebrity Culture* (2001) and *CyberRhythms: Black Innovations in Art and Technology* (2003). Her scholarship is primarily on the topics of race and American visual and artistic culture. Over the years, she has received several grants to conduct ongoing research on the nineteenth-century sculptor Edmonia Lewis. Her present research concentrates on early-twentieth-century race films and ethnicity films, as well as other instances of segregated art practice in the United States. A doctoral candidate at the University of Chicago, Crawford is completing her dissertation, entitled "The Practice of Ghetto: African-American and Jewish 'Race Films' from the 1920s."

Makeba G. Dixon-Hill is a graduate student in the Arts Administration and Policy Program at the School of the Art Institute of Chicago. In her recent role as curatorial assistant at the Spelman College Museum of Fine Art, she worked on this exhibition. After graduating with degrees in English and art history from Spelman College in 2003, Dixon-Hill participated in the first annual David C. Driskell Summer Arts Institute at the University of Maryland, College Park. From 2003 to 2006, she served as education and public programs coordinator, assisting in the development and implementation of adult programs at the Studio Museum in Harlem. At present, she is managing editor of *Code Z,* an online magazine dedicated to black visual culture. As a freelance writer, she has contributed to various visual and literary arts publications.

Merrill Falkenberg, PhD, is curator at the Aldrich Contemporary Art Museum, in Ridgefield, Conn. Before that, she was curator of art at the Parrish Art Museum, in Southampton, New York, where she cocurated *All the More Real: Portrayals of Intimacy and Empathy,* with Eric Fischl. Falkenberg was also an associate curator at the San Jose Museum of Art and has taught art history at both the San Francisco Art Institute and Vassar College. She has lectured widely on contemporary art, and published a number of catalogues and reviews. She has also completed several research assistantships at the Metropolitan Museum of Art, Whitney Museum of American Art, and Art Institute of Chicago. She received her doctorate from Stanford University, where she wrote a dissertation on interactivity and video art.

Leslie King-Hammond, PhD, completed her doctoral degree in art history at Johns Hopkins University. In 1976, she was appointed dean of graduate studies at Maryland Institute College of Art. In addition to being a member of the art history faculty, she has served on several juries, boards, organizations, and art commissions, including the advisory board, Edna Manley School for the Visual Arts, Kingston, Jamaica (1988–present); trustee, Baltimore Museum of Art (1981–87); Alvin Ailey Dance Theatre Foundation of Maryland (1991–94); president, College Art Association (1996–98); vice president, board of overseers, Baltimore School for the Arts (1996–99); vice president, Jacob Lawrence Catalogue Raisonné project (1996–2000); and the executive board, International Association of Art Critics (2000–2003). *Three Generations of African American Women Artists: A Study in Paradox* (1996), *Sugar and Spice: The Art of Betye Saar* (2003), *The Art of Aminah Robinson* (2003), and *The Many Faces of Beverly McIver* (2004) are some of the exhibition projects with which she has been involved. She is currently chair of the board of the Reginald F. Lewis Museum of Maryland African American History and

Culture, in Baltimore, and a board member of the Alliance of Artist Communities. In 2009, Pomegranate Press will publish her monograph on Hughie Lee-Smith.

Lowery Stokes Sims, PhD, is curator at the Museum of Arts & Design, New York. From 2000 to 2007, she served as executive director, then president, of the Studio Museum in Harlem, and, most recently, as adjunct curator for its permanent collection. Sims was on the education and curatorial staff of the Metropolitan Museum of Art from 1972 to 1999; in 1997, she organized a survey of the work of Richard Pousette-Dart. A specialist in modern and contemporary art, she is known particularly for her expertise on African, Latino, Native American, and Asian American artists. Her research on the Afro-Cuban Chinese surrealist artist Wifredo Lam was published in 2002 by the University of Texas Press. Sims has lectured nationally and internationally and guest-curated numerous exhibitions—most recently at the National Gallery, Kingston, Jamaica (2004), Cleveland Museum of Art (2006), and New-York Historical Society (2006). She is both catalogue editor and essayist for the National Museum of the American Indian's 2008 retrospective on Fritz Scholder. In 2003–4, Sims served on the jury for the World Trade Center memorial, and between 2004 and 2006 was chair of the Cultural Institutions Group, a coalition of museums, zoos, botanical gardens, and performing organizations funded by the City of New York. In 2005 and 2006, she was visiting professor at Queens College and Hunter College, New York; in spring 2007, a fellow at the Clark Art Institute; and in fall 2007, visiting professor in the department of art at the University of Minnesota, Twin Cities. Sims recently served on the advisory committee of the New York Cultural Innovation Fund of the Rockefeller Foundation.

Anne Collins Smith is curator of collections at the Spelman College Museum of Fine Art. She was the Andrew W. Mellon Curatorial Fellow at the Davis Museum and Cultural Center at Wellesley College, where she implemented interdisciplinary interpretation and programming related to the museum's permanent collection and exhibitions. During her tenure, she organized the exhibition *The Space Between: Artists Engaging Race and Syncretism,* which explored how artists across the African Diaspora engage and bring into accord their multipartite heritages and identities. An alumna of Spelman College, Smith completed her BA in English and art history in 1996; in 1998, she completed her MA in visual arts administration at New York University. Her research interests include cosmopolitanism and African diasporic continuity in artistic and cultural practices. She has served as an intern at the Cinque Gallery, in New York (1997–99), and as a Romare Bearden Fellow at the Saint Louis Art Museum (1999–2000).

INDEX

Note: Page numbers in *italics* denote locations of works illustrated in the text, or locations of illustrations of work by a particular artist.

Distributed by University of Washington Press
PO Box 50096
Seattle, WA 98145-5096
www.washington.edu/uwpress

Edited by Gerald Zeigerman
Proofread by Jessica Eber and Marie Weiler
Designed by Zach Hooker
Typeset by Maggie Lee
Indexed by Katherine Jensen
Produced by Marquand Books, Inc., Seattle
www.marquand.com
Color management by iocolor, Seattle
Printed and bound in China by Regent Publishing Services, Ltd.

Cinema Remixed & Reloaded: Black Women Artists and the Moving Image Since 1970 is coorganized by the Contemporary Arts Museum Houston and the Spelman College Museum of Fine Art, Atlanta.

The exhibition was presented in two parts at the Spelman College Museum of Fine Art, in Atlanta (September 14–December 8, 2007, and January 24–May 24, 2008), and at the Contemporary Arts Museum Houston (October 18, 2008–January 4, 2009).

Library of Congress Cataloging-in-Publication Data

Brownlee, Andrea Barnwell.
    Cinema remixed & reloaded : Black women artists and the moving image since 1970 / Andrea Barnwell Brownlee, Valerie Cassel Oliver.
        p. cm.
    Issued in connection with an exhibition coorganized by the Contemporary Arts Museum, Houston, and the Spelman College Museum of Fine Art, Atlanta.
    Includes bibliographical references and index.
    ISBN 978-0-295-98864-1 (hardcover: alk. paper)
    1. Video art—Exhibitions. 2. Women artists, Black—Exhibitions. I. Oliver, Valerie Cassel. II. Contemporary Arts Museum. III. Spelman College. Museum of Fine Art. IV. Title. V. Title: Cinema remixed & reloaded.
N6494.V53B76 2008
778.59082—dc22   2008021942

Front cover: Elizabeth Axtman, stills from *American Classics*, 2005 (see p. 94)
Back cover: Howardena Pindell, stills from *Free, White and 21*, 1980 (see p. 126)
Endsheets: Yvonne Welbon, stills from *Monique*, 1991 (see p. 141)
Page 1: Barbara McCullough, stills from *Water Ritual #1: An Urban Rite of Purification,* 1979 (p. 118)
Page 3: Cauleen Smith, stills from *The Changing Same,* 1998–2001 (see p. 135)